Let's Study!

The
Grammar
School

예비
중학

Iam books

Contents

Features

새로운 중학교 교과 과정 반영
자기주도 학습을 통한 내신 완벽 대비
내신 기출문제 분석
명확한 핵심 문법 해설
Workbook - 다양하고 풍부한 문법문제 수록

Unit 문법 설명

· 새로운 교과 과정이 반영된 교과서를 분석하여 꼭 알아야 할 문법 사항을 예문과 함께 정리하였습니다.

· 쉬운 설명으로 문법의 기초를 다질 수 있습니다.

Practice

· 다양한 주관식 문법 문제를 통해 배운 문법 사항을 문제로 풀어보며 익히도록 하였습니다.

· 핵심 문법 설명을 토대로 배운 문법 사항을 Practice를 통해 확실하게 점검할 수 있습니다.

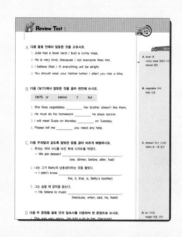

Review Test 1

· 해당 Chapter에서 배운 문법 사항을 통합하여 다양한 주관식 문제를 통해 복습하며 점검하도록 하였습니다.

· 학습 내용을 바탕으로 문제를 해결하며 응용력을 키울 수 있도록 하였습니다.

Review Test 2

· 해당 Chapter에서 배운 내용들을 학교 시험 유형으로 구성하였으며 출제 비율이 높은 문제를 선별하여 종합 문제로 제시하였습니다.

· 학교 시험에 나올만한 내신 대비 문제와 주관식 문제를 수록하여 내신을 완벽하게 대비하도록 하였습니다.

· 종합문제를 통해 자신의 실력을 점검하도록 하였습니다.

Workbook

· 해당 Chapter에서 배운 문법 사항과 관련된 추가 문법 문제로 구성하였습니다.

· 주관식 문제를 대폭 수록하여 많은 문제를 풀어보며 실력을 쌓을 수 있도록 하였습니다.

문장의 구성 요소

1. 8품사

*품사 : 성질이나 문법적 역할이 같은 단어끼리 모아 놓은 것을 품사라고 한다.

(1) 명사 : 사람, 동물, 사물, 장소나 개념 등을 나타내는 말로, 문장에서 주어, 목적어, 보어로 쓰인다.
    ① 셀 수 있는 명사
       – 보통명사 : 하나씩 구분할 수 있는 명사(cat, chair, house 등)
       – 집합명사 : 사람이나 사물이 여럿 모여 집합체를 이루는 명사(family, team 등)
    ② 셀 수 없는 명사
       – 고유명사 : 이름이나 지명 등 세상에 하나밖에 없는 명사(Korea, Sunday 등)
       – 물질명사 : 모양이나 크기가 없는 물질이나 재료로 이루어진 명사(water, air 등)
       – 추상명사 : 모양이 없이 추상적인 개념을 나타내는 명사(love, happiness 등)

(2) 대명사 : 사람이나 사물의 이름을 대신하는 말로, 문장에서 주어, 목적어, 보어로 쓰인다.
    ① 인칭대명사 : 사람이나 동물, 사물을 대신하여 나타내는 말(I, me, my, mine 등)
    ② 지시대명사 : '이것' 또는 '저것'이라고 대상을 가리키는 말(this, that 등)

(3) 동사 : 사람, 동물, 사물의 동작이나 상태를 나타내는 말이다.
    ① be동사 : '~이다, ~에 있다'라는 뜻을 나타내는 동사(am, are, is 등)
    ② 일반동사 : 동작이나 상태를 나타내는 대부분의 동사(go, see, eat 등)
    ③ 조동사 : be동사나 일반동사 앞에서 동사의 뜻을 더해 주는 동사(can, will 등)

(4) 형용사 : 사람이나 사물의 성질, 성격, 상태 등을 나타내는 말이다.(good, pretty, red, tall 등)

(5) 부사 : 방법, 정도 등을 나타내며 동사, 형용사, 부사 또는 문장 전체를 꾸며 주는 말이다.(very, really, late, early 등)

(6) 전치사 : 명사나 대명사 앞에 쓰이며 장소, 시간, 목적, 수단 등을 나타내는 말이다.(in, on, under, by, at, to, from 등)

(7) 접속사 : 단어와 단어, 구와 구, 절과 절을 이어주는 말이다.(and, but, so 등)

(8) 감탄사 : 기쁨, 슬픔, 놀람 등의 감정을 나타내는 말이다.(oh, wow, ouch 등)

2. 문장의 구조

(1) 주부와 술부

① 주부 : '~은/는, ~이/가'에 해당하는 주어를 포함한 부분을 주부라고 한다. 주부는 주어만으로 이루어질 때도 있고 수식어구를 포함할 때도 있다.

The woman is a doctor. 그 여자는 의사이다.

The woman on the chair is a doctor. 그 의자에 앉아 있는 여자는 의사이다.

② 술부 : '~이다, ~하다'에 해당하는 동사를 포함한 부분을 술부라고 한다. 술부는 동사만으로 이루어질 때도 있고 목적어, 보어, 수식어구를 포함할 때도 있다.

I eat. 나는 먹는다.

I eat an apple. 나는 사과를 먹는다.

I eat an apple in the park. 나는 공원에서 사과를 먹는다.

＊주어 : 동사의 주체가 되는 말

＊동사 : 주어의 상태나 동작을 나타내는 말

＊목적어 : 동작의 대상이 되는 말

＊보어 : 주어나 목적어의 성질이나 상태를 나타내는 말

(2) 구와 절

① 구 : 「주어+동사」를 포함하지 않은 둘 이상의 단어가 모여 명사, 형용사, 부사의 역할을 하는 것을 말한다.

– 명사구(명사 역할) : I enjoy eating pizza. (목적어)

– 형용사구(형용사 역할) : The cat on the sofa is cute. (명사 수식)

– 부사구(부사 역할) : I put the car in the garage. (동사 수식)

② 절 : 「주어+동사」를 포함한 둘 이상의 단어가 문장의 일부를 이루는 것을 말한다.

He is tall, but his brother is short. 그는 키가 크지만 그의 형은 키가 작다.

＊절도 구처럼 명사, 형용사, 부사의 역할을 한다.

– 명사절 : I know that he is honest. (목적어)

– 형용사절 : The man who is sitting on the chair is Tom. (명사 수식)

– 부사절 : Let's meet tomorrow if you are busy now. (문장 전체 수식)

be동사란 무엇인가?
be동사는 직접 동작을 나타내지는 않지만, 주어의 성질이나 성격, 상태를 나타낼 때 사용한다. be동사는 주어의 수와 인칭에 따라서 형태가 다르며 '～이다, ～하다, ～ (에) 있다'라는 뜻이다.

대명사란 무엇인가?
대명사는 명사를 대신하여 나타내는 말로 인칭대명사, 지시대명사, 소유대명사가 있다. 인칭대명사는 인칭과 수에 따라서 형태가 다르며 주격, 목적격, 소유격에 맞게 알맞은 형태로 사용해야 한다. 지시대명사는 사물이나 사람을 가리킬 때 사용한다.

Chapter 1. be동사와 대명사

01 be동사의 현재형과 과거형

1. be동사

· be동사는 '～이다, (상태가) ～하다, (～에) 있다'의 뜻으로 주어의 인칭(1, 2, 3인칭)과 수(단수, 복수)에 따라 am, are, is를 쓴다.

I **am** a student. 나는 학생이다.   He **is** clever. 그는 똑똑하다.

We **are** in the park. 우리는 그 공원에 있다.

＊be동사 뒤에 명사가 오면 '～이다'라는 뜻이고, 장소를 나타내는 전치사가 오면 '～에 있다'라는 뜻이다. 또한 be동사 뒤에 형용사가 오면 '～하다'라는 뜻이다.

	단수(축약형)	복수(축약형)
1인칭	I am(I'm)	We are(We're)
2인칭	You are(You're)	You are(You're)
3인칭	He is(He's) She is(She's) It is(It's)	They are(They're)

＊Amy, a dog, Korea 등 1인칭과 2인칭이 아닌 것은 모두 3인칭이다.

＊셀 수 있는 것이 하나이면 단수, 둘 이상이면 복수라고 한다.

Check 1 다음 괄호 안에서 알맞은 것을 고르시오.

1. I (am / are) happy.

2. They (is / are) very tall.

3. He (is / am) my brother.

---

2. be동사의 과거형

· be동사의 과거형은 '～이었다, (상태가) ～했다, (～에) 있었다'의 뜻으로 주어의 수와 인칭에 따라 was나 were를 쓴다.

I **was** at home yesterday. 나는 어제 집에 있었다.

He **was** twelve years old last year. 그는 작년에 12살이었다.

They **were** late for school. 그들은 학교에 지각했다.

＊과거형은 주로 과거를 나타내는 말(yesterday, last, ago 등)과 함께 쓰인다.

	단수	복수
1인칭	I was	We were
2인칭	You were	You were
3인칭	He was She was It was	They were

Check 2 다음 괄호 안에서 알맞은 것을 고르시오.

1. She (was / were) sad last week.

2. We (was / were) good students.

3. I (was / were) very angry yesterday.

Practice 1　다음 괄호 안에서 알맞은 것을 고르시오.

1. (He / They / I) are very busy.

2. She (am / are / is) beautiful.

3. We (am / are / is) in the room.

4. (I / They / She) is a very cute girl.

5. I (am / are / is) hungry now.

6. Your books (am / are / is) on the table.

7. They (am / are / is) kind to people.

 Practice 2　다음 밑줄 친 부분을 줄여 문장을 다시 쓰시오.

1. It is a great idea.　　　　→ _____

2. He is late for the party.　→ _____

3. They are good singers.　　→ _____

4. We are in the kitchen.　　→ _____

5. I am a good doctor.　　　→ _____

6. You are my best friend.　　→ _____

7. She is fourteen years old.　→ _____

Practice 3　다음 괄호 안의 단어를 주어로 바꿔 문장을 다시 쓰시오.

1. He is a soccer player. (I)　→ _____

2. They were very big. (it)　　→ _____

3. I was angry at you. (we)　→ _____

4. It is on the desk. (they)　　→ _____

5. I was at the station. (he)　→ _____

6. You are smart. (she)　　　→ _____

7. He was very tired. (you)　→ _____

Words　busy 바쁜　cute 귀여운　idea 생각, 개념　kitchen 부엌　player 운동선수　smart 영리한　tired 지친

11

02 be동사의 부정문과 의문문

1. be동사의 부정문

· be동사의 부정문은 「주어+be동사+not ~.」의 형태로 '~이 아니다, ~이 없다'의 뜻이다.

I am **not**[I'm not] happy. 나는 행복하지 않다.

You're **not**[You aren't] tall. 너는 키가 크지 않다.

She's **not**[She isn't] a teacher. 그녀는 선생님이 아니다.

It's **not**[It isn't] small. 그것은 작지 않다.

They're **not**[They aren't] from Japan. 그들은 일본 출신이 아니다.

* is not은 isn't로, are not은 aren't로 줄여 쓴다. am not은 amn't로 줄여 쓰지 않는다.

  I am not → I'm not

He was **not**[He wasn't] in his room. 그는 그의 방에 있지 않았다.

We were **not**[We weren't] hungry. 우리는 배고프지 않았다.

* 과거형의 경우는 '~이 아니었다, ~이 없었다'라는 뜻이다.

Check 1 다음 중 not이 들어갈 알맞은 위치를 고르시오.

1. He (①) is (②) a (③) nice (④) student.
2. They (①) were (②) in (③) the kitchen (④).
3. You (①) are (②) my (③) friend (④).

---

2. be동사의 의문문

· be동사의 의문문은 「Be동사+주어 ~?」의 형태로 '~이니?, ~이 있니?'의 뜻이다.

She is happy. 그녀는 행복하다. (평서문)

→ **Is she** happy? 그녀는 행복하니? (의문문)

* 주어와 be동사의 위치를 바꾸고 문장 뒤에 물음표를 붙인다.
* 과거형의 경우에는 '~이었니?, ~이 있었니?'라는 뜻이다.

· be동사의 의문문에 대한 대답은 긍정이면 「Yes, 주어+be동사.」, 부정이면 「No, 주어+be동사+not.」으로 한다.

Are you hungry? 너는 배가 고프니? – Yes, I am. / No, I'm not.

Is she your sister? 그녀는 너의 여동생이니? – Yes, she is. / No, she isn't.

Were they in the park? 그들은 공원에 있었니? – Yes, they were. / No, they weren't.

* 부정의 대답은 「be동사+not」의 축약형으로 나타낸다.

Check 2 다음 괄호 안의 단어를 바르게 배열하여 의문문을 만드시오.

1. (he, is, an actor)?   → _____
2. (are, tired, you)?   → _____
3. (she, at home, was)? → _____

다음 괄호 안의 단어를 바르게 배열하여 문장을 완성하시오.

1. (she, not, is) an actress. → _____

2. (were, not, they) in the bookstore. → _____

3. (not, is, he) absent from school. → _____

4. Alice (is, a, not) teacher. → _____

5. (Julie, in, is, the classroom, ?) → _____

6. (your sneakers, new, are, ?) → _____

7. (was, the book, interesting, ?) → _____

다음 문장을 괄호 안의 지시대로 바꿔 쓰시오.

1. I'm very tired and sleepy. (부정문으로) → _____

2. Lisa was a famous painter. (의문문으로) → _____

3. He was in his office. (부정문으로) → _____

4. They are good friends. (의문문으로) → _____

5. My clothes were dirty. (의문문으로) → _____

6. The game is very exciting. (의문문으로) → _____

7. We are in the bookstore. (부정문으로) → _____

다음 질문에 긍정은 Yes, 부정은 No를 이용하여 알맞은 답을 쓰시오.

1. Are you a farmer? (긍정) → _____

2. Is he from Canada? (부정) → _____

3. Were they at school? (긍정) → _____

4. Was she a dentist? (부정) → _____

5. Is your sister tall? (긍정) → _____

6. Are they on the second floor? (부정) → _____

7. Was his mother in the market? (긍정) → _____

 Words actress 여배우 absent 결석한 sneakers 운동화 famous 유명한 dirty 더러운 dentist 치과 의사

03 인칭대명사와 명사의 소유격

1. 인칭대명사

· 인칭대명사는 사람이나 동물, 사물을 대신하여 가리키는 말로 인칭, 수, 격에 따라 형태가 달라진다.

She is a pianist. 그녀는 피아니스트이다. (주격)

My father teaches **them**. 나의 아버지는 그들을 가르친다. (목적격)

Jane is **my** sister. Jane은 나의 여동생이다. (소유격)

This umbrella is **yours**. 이 우산은 너의 것이다. (소유대명사)

＊주격 : 문장에서 주어로 쓰이며 '~은, 는, 이, 가'의 뜻이다.

＊목적격 : 문장에서 목적어로 쓰이며 '~을, ~에게'의 뜻이다.

＊소유격 : '~의'라는 뜻으로 소유를 나타낸다.

＊소유대명사 : '~의 것'이라는 뜻으로 「소유격+명사」를 대신한다.

	단수				복수			
	주격	목적격	소유격	소유대명사	주격	목적격	소유격	소유대명사
1인칭	I	me	my	mine	we	us	our	ours
2인칭	you	you	your	yours	you	you	your	yours
3인칭	he	him	his	his	they	them	their	theirs
	she	her	her	hers				
	it	it	its	−				

> **Check 1 다음 밑줄 친 부분을 인칭대명사로 바꿔 쓰시오.**
>
> 1. Jack is a doctor.
> 2. Willy and I are from London.
> 3. The castle is old.

2. 명사의 소유격

· 사람이나 동물의 소유격 : 「명사+'s」

This is **Jenny's** camera. 이것은 Jenny의 카메라이다.

A **pig's** tail is short and curly. 돼지의 꼬리는 짧고 동그랗게 말려 있다.

· 사물이나 장소의 소유격 : 「of+명사」

The roof **of the house** is blue. 그 집의 지붕은 파란색이다.

The name **of that park** is Bronx. 저 공원의 이름은 Bronx이다.

> **Check 2 다음 괄호 안에서 알맞은 것을 고르시오.**
>
> 1. It's (Nick's / Nicks) book.
> 2. She is my (mother / mother's) sister.
> 3. The (bird's / birds) wings are beautiful.

다음 밑줄 친 부분을 인칭대명사로 바꿔 쓰시오.

1. <u>Sarah</u> is a cook. → _____

2. <u>The hippo</u> is big. → _____

3. <u>She and I</u> are in the park. → _____

4. <u>The pencils</u> are long. → _____

5. <u>The children</u> are at the zoo. → _____

6. <u>My father</u> is very kind. → _____

7. <u>The girl</u> isn't sleepy. → _____

Practice 2 다음 밑줄 친 부분을 바르게 고치시오.

1. Soccer is <u>me</u> favorite sport. → _____

2. This red bike is <u>her</u>. → _____

3. I don't know <u>yours</u> address. → _____

4. This is <u>hers</u> cousin. → _____

5. Our cat is small, and <u>their</u> is big. → _____

6. They are not her dolls. They are <u>him</u>. → _____

7. Your hair is black, and <u>my</u> is brown. → _____

Practice 3 다음 우리말과 같은 뜻이 되도록 빈칸에 알맞은 말을 쓰시오.

1. 이것은 Leo의 우산이다. → This is _____ umbrella.

2. 저것은 Brad의 집이다. → That is _____ house.

3. 돼지의 다리는 짧다. → A _____ legs are short.

4. 이것들은 내 남동생의 바지이다. → These are my _____ pants.

5. 로마는 이탈리아의 수도이다. → Rome is the capital _____ Italy.

6. 그 책의 제목은 소나기이다. → The title _____ the book is *Rain Shower*.

7. Emily는 그 게임의 우승자이다. → Emily is the winner _____ the game.

Words cook 요리사   zoo 동물원   address 주소   pants 바지   capital 수도   title 제목   winner 승자

04 지시대명사와 it의 쓰임

1. 지시대명사

• 지시대명사는 사물이나 사람을 가리키는 대명사로 this, that, these, those가 있다.

가리키는 대상	단수	복수
가까이 있는 사물이나 사람	this(이것, 이 사람)	these(이것들, 이 사람들)
떨어져 있는 사물이나 사람	that(저것, 저 사람)	those(저것들, 저 사람들)

• 의문문에서 this나 that으로 물으면 it으로, these나 those로 물으면 they로 대답한다.

Is this your bag? – Yes, **it is**. / No, **it isn't**.
이것은 너의 가방이니? – 응, 그래. / 아니, 그렇지 않아.

Are those your books? – Yes, **they are**. / No, **they aren't**.
저것들은 너의 책들이니? – 응, 그래. / 아니, 그렇지 않아.

• this, that, these, those는 뒤에 오는 명사를 수식하는 지시형용사로도 쓰이며, 이때는 '이 ～'
또는 '저 ～'의 뜻으로 쓰인다.

This movie is very interesting. 이 영화는 매우 재미있다.

These shoes are pretty. 이 신발은 예쁘다.

> **Check 1** 다음 괄호 안에서 알맞은 것을 고르시오.
>
> 1. (This / These) is my friend, Billy.
> 2. Look at (that / those) monkeys.
> 3. Are (this / these) your clothes?

2. it의 쓰임

• 대명사 it은 앞에서 언급된 것을 가리키는 말로 '그것'이라는 뜻이다.

I play baseball. I like **it**. 나는 야구를 한다. 나는 그것을 좋아한다.

• 비인칭 주어 it은 시간, 날짜, 요일, 날씨, 계절, 거리, 명암 등을 나타낼 때 문장의 주어로 쓴다.
이때 it은 특별한 의미가 없으므로 '그것'이라고 해석하지 않는다.

시간	It is three o'clock. 3시이다.
날짜	It is December 2nd. 12월 2일이다.
요일	It is Monday today. 오늘은 월요일이다.
날씨	It is snowy. 눈이 온다.
계절	It is spring now. 지금은 봄이다.
거리	It is four kilometers. 4km이다.
명암	It is bright outside. 밖은 밝다.

> **Check 2** 다음 밑줄 친 it이 대명사인지 비인칭 주어인지 고르시오.
>
> 1. It's your jacket. (대명사 / 비인칭 주어)
> 2. It's raining outside. (대명사 / 비인칭 주어)
> 3. It's Sunday today. (대명사 / 비인칭 주어)

Practice 1 다음 괄호 안에서 알맞은 것을 고르시오.

1. (This / These) are my shoes.

2. (That / Those) is Tim's cap.

3. Are (this / these) your sisters?

4. (That / Those) boys are very thirsty.

5. This (is / are) his cell phone.

6. (Is / Are) these Eric's cameras?

7. I like (that / those) blouse.

Practice 2 다음 문장을 지시형용사를 이용하여 바꿔 쓰시오.

1. This is a big house.   → This house _____.

2. Those are old buildings. → _____

3. That is an exciting game. → _____

4. Those are new dresses.   → _____

5. That is a great movie.   → _____

6. This is a smart girl.   → _____

7. These are fast runners.   → _____

Practice 3 다음 우리말과 같도록 빈칸에 알맞은 말을 쓰시오.

1. 지금은 봄이다.   → _____ is _____ now.

2. 오늘은 3월 2일이다.   → _____ _____ March 2nd today.

3. 오늘은 화창합니까?   → _____ it _____ today?

4. 8시 정각이다.   → _____ _____ eight o'clock.

5. 학교까지 20분이 걸린다.   → _____ takes 20 _____ to school.

6. 그 강까지 1킬로미터이다. → _____ _____ one kilometer to the river.

7. 밖이 매우 어둡다.   → _____ is very _____ outside.

Words thirsty 목마른   blouse 블라우스   building 건물   runner 주자   minute 분   dark 어두운   outside 밖에

17

A. 다음 빈칸에 알맞은 말을 〈보기〉에서 골라 쓰시오.

> 〈보기〉 are   they're   it's   is   were   am

1. We _____ very busy last weekend.

2. He _____ a pilot. She is a police officer.

3. _____ you sleepy now?

4. Look at that picture. _____ very wonderful.

B. 다음 괄호 안의 지시대로 문장을 바꿔 쓰시오.

1. They are my grandparents. (부정문으로)

   → _____

2. James was in London two weeks ago. (의문문으로)

   → _____

3. I'm a famous musician. (부정문으로)

   → _____

4. You were in the same class last year. (의문문으로)

   → _____

C. 다음 밑줄 친 부분을 바르게 고치시오.

1. Is <u>him</u> your classmate?

2. I know <u>Mary</u> phone number.

3. The yellow skirt is <u>my</u>. That blue shirt is <u>her</u>.

4. Are the albums yours? – Yes, <u>it is</u>.

D. 다음 우리말과 같도록 괄호 안의 단어를 이용하여 문장을 완성하시오.

1. 이분은 나의 수학 선생님이시다. (this, math, teacher)

   → _____

2. 저 소녀들은 Eric의 여자 형제들이다. (those, Eric's, sisters)

   → _____

3. 이것들은 너의 고양이들이니? (these, cats, your)

   → _____

4. 여름에는 덥다. (it, hot, summer)

   → _____

Words

A. last 지난
pilot 조종사
wonderful 멋진

B. ago ~ 전에
musician 음악가
same 같은, 동일한

C. classmate 반 친구
phone number 전화번호
album 앨범, 사진첩

D. math 수학
hot 더운
summer 여름

1. 다음 두 단어의 관계가 나머지와 <u>다른</u> 것은?

　① I – me 　　　　② they – them
　③ she – her 　　　④ he – him
　⑤ we – our

2. 다음 중 밑줄 친 부분을 줄여 쓸 수 <u>없는</u> 것은?

　① <u>You are</u> very smart.
　② I <u>am not</u> a student.
　③ <u>It is</u> my ball.
　④ <u>She is</u> very pretty.
　⑤ We <u>are not</u> in the library.

3. 다음 중 밑줄 친 부분의 쓰임이 <u>잘못된</u> 것은?

　① <u>Are</u> you sad?
　② She <u>was</u> a doctor.
　③ We <u>are</u> late for school.
　④ <u>Were</u> they at the concert?
　⑤ Bob <u>are</u> eleven years old.

4. 다음 중 의문문으로 바르게 고친 것은?

　① You are thirsty.
　　→ You thirsty are?
　② He is a good teacher.
　　→ Is a good teacher he?
　③ They are soccer players.
　　→ Are soccer players they?
　④ Ann is your sister.
　　→ Is Ann your sister?
　⑤ She and her son are tall.
　　→ Are she tall and her son?

5. 다음 빈칸에 알맞지 <u>않은</u> 것은?

> Amy was in the hospital _____ .

　① yesterday 　　　② last week
　③ a month ago 　　④ last year
　⑤ now

6. 다음 빈칸에 알맞은 것은?

> I love _____ very much.

　① his 　　　　　② she
　③ them 　　　　 ④ your
　⑤ its

7. 다음 밑줄 친 부분의 쓰임이 나머지와 <u>다른</u> 것은?

　① <u>It</u>'s not far from here.
　② <u>It</u>'s snowing now.
　③ <u>It</u>'s bright outside.
　④ <u>It</u>'s a very funny story.
　⑤ <u>It</u>'s Monday today.

8. 다음 대화의 빈칸에 들어갈 말이 순서대로 짝지어 진 것을 고르시오.

> A: _____ cars are very old.
> B: Yes, but _____ car is not old.

　① Those – these 　　② This – that
　③ These – that 　　　④ That – those
　⑤ That – these

9. 다음 중 빈칸에 aren't가 들어갈 수 없는 것은?

① You _____ happy.

② He and I _____ from Japan.

③ These _____ my cameras.

④ The boys _____ in the zoo.

⑤ The computer _____ expensive.

10. 다음 중 어법상 어색한 것은?

① She's from Canada.

② Judy is his aunt.

③ It is rainy today.

④ These are my pants.

⑤ Her is my best friend.

11. 다음 빈칸에 들어갈 수 있는 것은?

_____ is my sister.

① We   ② Jenny

③ Those   ④ They

⑤ Ann and Tom

12. 다음 빈칸에 공통으로 알맞은 것은?

· They _____ my grandparents.

· These cookies _____ Jane's.

① am   ② is

③ are   ④ isn't

⑤ was

[13-14] 다음 중 어법상 자연스러운 것은?

13. ① Are they hungry?

② Is she and he tall?

③ Is you in the classroom?

④ Are she your sisters?

⑤ Are her father at home?

14. ① Those tree is short.

② This cats are cute.

③ I like these photos.

④ That is my socks.

⑤ Those are your key.

15. 다음 문장을 부정문으로 바르게 고친 것은?

He is kind and smart.

① He not is kind and smart.

② He isn't kind and smart.

③ He is kind and smart not.

④ He is kind not and smart.

⑤ He is kind and not smart.

16. 다음 중 밑줄 친 부분이 어색한 것은?

① Her dress is pretty.

② These are ours books.

③ He is a smart boy.

④ We know his house.

⑤ Wash your hands first.

일반동사란 무엇인가?

동사는 주어의 동작이나 상태를 나타내는 말로 be동사, 조동사,
일반동사가 있는데 be동사와 조동사를 제외한 모든 동사가 일반
동사이다. 일반동사는 인칭과 수에 따라 형태가 변한다.

일반동사의 과거형은 어떻게 나타내는가?

지금 일어나고 있는 일을 현재라고 하고 앞으로 일어날 일을 미
래라고 하며 지나간 일을 과거라고 한다. 이때, 과거의 일을 나
타내기 위해서는 과거형 동사를 사용하여 과거 문장을 나타낸다.
일반동사의 과거형은 보통 일반동사에 -ed를 붙여서 만든다.

Chapter 2. 일반동사

Unit 05. 일반동사의 의미와 형태

Unit 06. 일반동사의 과거형

Unit 07. 일반동사의 부정문과 의문문

05 일반동사의 의미와 형태

1. 일반동사

·일반동사는 be동사와 조동사를 제외한 모든 동사로 주어의 동작이나 상태를 나타낸다.

I **am** a student. (be동사) I **go** to school. (일반동사) I **can** speak English. (조동사)
나는 학생이다. 나는 학교에 간다. 나는 영어를 말할 수 있다.

	의미	예
be동사	~이다, ~하다, ~(에) 있다	am, are, is
조동사	~할 수 있다, ~할 것이다, ~해야 한다	can, will, must
일반동사	~하다(동작, 상태)	do, go, come, sing, like 등

Check 1 일반동사가 쓰인 문장이면 ○표, 그렇지 않으면 ×표 하시오.

　　1. She is my mother.　　　　　(　　　)

　　2. I like apples very much.　　(　　　)

　　3. Dean and I go to the park.　(　　　)

2. 일반동사의 현재형

·일반동사의 현재형은 동사원형을 그대로 쓰는데, 주어가 3인칭 단수인 경우에는 동사원형의 끝에 -s나 -es를 붙인다.

I **want** a blue ball. 나는 파란색 공을 원한다.

She **wants** some cookies. 그녀는 약간의 쿠키를 원한다.

* 현재형은 현재의 사실이나 상태, 반복되는 동작이나 습관을 나타낸다.

* 3인칭 단수 : 1인칭과 2인칭을 제외한 모든 명사는 3인칭인데, 그 중 단수를 의미한다.

3. 일반동사의 3인칭 단수 현재형

·일반동사의 3인칭 단수 현재형 만드는 방법

대부분의 동사	동사원형+-s	want → wants, work → works, see → sees, like → likes, sing → sings, come → comes
-o, -x, -(s)s, -sh, -ch 로 끝나는 동사	동사원형+-es	go → goes, mix → mixes, pass → passes, wash → washes, teach → teaches
「자음+y」로 끝나는 동사	y를 i로 고치고 +-es	study → studies, cry → cries, fly → flies
「모음+y」로 끝나는 동사	동사원형+-s	buy → buys, play → plays, stay → stays

불규칙 변화 동사	have → has

Check 2 다음 일반동사의 3인칭 단수형을 쓰시오.

　　1. fix　　→ _____　　　2. walk　→ _____

　　3. have　→ _____　　　4. read　→ _____

Practice 1 다음 괄호 안에서 알맞은 것을 고르시오.

1. I (like / likes) my toy cars.

2. The concert (start / starts) at eight o'clock.

3. My father (work / works) at a hospital.

4. Peter (live / lives) in Chicago.

5. They (read / reads) many books.

6. She (play / plays) the violin after school.

7. My sister and I (listen / listens) to music.

Practice 2 다음 밑줄 친 부분을 현재형으로 바르게 고치시오.

1. Ann <u>study</u> Japanese.   → _____

2. She <u>do</u> her homework.   → _____

3. Kate <u>help</u> poor people.   → _____

4. My mother <u>teach</u> English.   → _____

5. He <u>come</u> from Canada.   → _____

6. A butterfly <u>have</u> beautiful wings. → _____

7. Jamie <u>watch</u> TV all day long.   → _____

Practice 3 다음 빈칸에 주어진 동사의 현재형을 쓰시오.

1. Anna _____ to school by bus. (go)

2. The baby _____ loudly. (cry)

3. Mark _____ the newspaper every day. (buy)

4. My father _____ the dishes after dinner. (do)

5. The man _____ his work. (finish)

6. Thomas _____ his car. (clean)

7. He _____ a new computer. (want)

 Words violin 바이올린   Japanese 일본어   wing 날개   loudly 크게   newspaper 신문

06 일반동사의 과거형

1. 일반동사의 과거형 : 규칙변화

· 과거의 일을 나타낼 때에는 일반동사의 과거형을 사용하여 나타낸다. 일반동사의 과거형은 일반적으로 동사원형+-ed를 붙여서 만든다.

We **clean** the room. 우리는 방을 청소한다. (현재형)

They **cleaned** the room yesterday. 그들은 어제 방을 청소했다. (과거형)

· 일반동사의 과거형 : 규칙변화

대부분의 동사	동사원형+-ed	watch → watched, help → helped
-e로 끝나는 동사	동사원형+-d	like → liked, love → loved
「자음+y」로 끝나는 동사	y를 i로 고치고+-ed	cry → cried, study → studied
「모음+y」로 끝나는 동사	동사원형+-ed	play → played, enjoy → enjoyed
「단모음+단자음」으로 끝나는 1음절 동사	마지막 자음을 한 번 더 쓰고+-ed	stop → stopped, plan → planned

Check 1 다음 밑줄 친 일반동사를 과거형으로 바꿔 쓰시오.

1. I <u>watch</u> movies in the room.
2. We <u>like</u> basketball.
3. The girl <u>plays</u> the piano.

2. 일반동사의 과거형 : 불규칙변화

· 일반동사의 과거형 : 불규칙변화

현재형과 과거형이 다른 동사			현재형과 과거형이 같은 동사
현재형 − 과거형	현재형 − 과거형	현재형 − 과거형	현재형 − 과거형
begin − began	give − gave	see − saw	cut − cut
buy − bought	go − went	sing − sang	hit − hit
come − came	have − had	sit − sat	hurt − hurt
do − did	lose − lost	swim − swam	let − let
eat − ate	make − made	take − took	put − put
find − found	meet − met	think − thought	read − read
get − got	run − ran	write − wrote	set − set

We **went** to the gallery last Sunday. 우리는 지난 일요일에 미술관에 갔었다.

My mother **bought** a scarf yesterday. 나의 어머니는 어제 스카프를 사셨다.

＊규칙적으로 변하는 동사들과 달리 불규칙으로 변하는 동사는 외워두는 것이 좋다.

Check 2 다음 일반동사의 과거형을 쓰시오.

1. take → _____   2. read → _____

3. eat → _____   4. buy → _____

Practice 1 다음 밑줄 친 부분을 바르게 고치시오.

1. The train stops here a few minutes ago. → _____

2. Karen was tired. She stays at home all day. → _____

3. Susan helps an old woman yesterday. → _____

4. We have fun at the concert last night. → _____

5. I meet Thomas and Bill last Saturday. → _____

6. He washes his car yesterday morning. → _____

7. He enjoys dinner at a restaurant yesterday. → _____

Practice 2 다음 빈칸에 주어진 동사의 과거형을 쓰시오.

1. He _____ a walk in the park. (take)

2. Chris and I _____ to the tree. (run)

3. They _____ on the grass. (sit)

4. Ann _____ a letter to her friend. (write)

5. My mother _____ back early. (come)

6. I _____ bread and milk for lunch. (eat)

7. She _____ her cell phone in the kitchen. (find)

Practice 3 다음 우리말과 같도록 빈칸에 알맞은 말을 쓰시오.

1. Sarah는 기타를 연주했다. → Sarah _____ the guitar.

2. Tony는 한 시간 동안 수영을 했다. → Tony _____ for an hour.

3. 나는 우산을 탁자 위에 놓았다. → I _____ an umbrella on the table.

4. Steve와 Mary는 함께 노래를 불렀다. → Steve and Mary _____ together.

5. David는 만화책을 읽었다. → David _____ a comic book.

6. 그녀는 어제 모자 하나를 만들었다. → She _____ a hat yesterday.

7. 그는 지하철에서 지갑을 잃어버렸다. → He _____ his purse on the subway.

Words stay 머무르다   restaurant 식당   grass 잔디, 풀   early 일찍   guitar 기타   purse 지갑   subway 지하철

25

07 일반동사의 부정문과 의문문

1. 현재형의 부정문과 의문문

· 일반동사의 부정문과 의문문을 만들 때 현재형에서는 do나 does를 사용하여 만든다.

	형태	예문
부정문	주어가 1, 2인칭 또는 복수일 때 → 주어+do not[don't]+동사원형 ~. 주어가 3인칭 단수일 때 → 주어+does not[doesn't]+동사원형 ~.	I walk my dog. → I **do not[don't]** walk my dog. He studies hard. → He **does not[doesn't]** study hard.
의문문	Do[Does]+주어+동사원형 ~? 대답 : Yes, 주어+do[does]. 〈긍정〉 　　　 No, 주어+don't[doesn't]. 〈부정〉 * 주어가 3인칭 단수일 경우에는 Do 대신 Does를 쓰며, 대답에서는 do나 don't 대신 does나 doesn't를 쓴다.	You need an umbrella. → **Do** you need an umbrella? 　– Yes, I do. / No, I don't. She has a new camera. → **Does** she have a new camera? 　– Yes, she does. / 　　No, she doesn't.

Check 1 다음 괄호 안에서 알맞은 것을 고르시오.

1. We (don't / doesn't) like the clothes.

2. Vicky (don't / doesn't) have a brother.

3. (Do / Does) she drink milk every morning?

2. 과거형의 부정문과 의문문

· 일반동사의 과거형 문장은 주어의 인칭과 상관없이 do의 과거형인 did를 사용하여 만든다.

	형태	예문
부정문	주어+did not+동사원형 ~.	I got up early then. → I **did not[didn't]** get up early then. She visited her uncle. → She **did not[didn't]** visit her uncle.
의문문	Did+주어+동사원형 ~? 대답 : Yes, 주어+did. 〈긍정〉 　　　 No, 주어+didn't. 〈부정〉	You met them in the park. → **Did** you meet them in the park? 　– Yes, I did. / No, I didn't. He played soccer last week. → **Did** he play soccer last week? 　– Yes, he did. / No, he didn't.

Check 2 다음 문장을 괄호 안의 지시대로 바꾸시오.

1. She bought a new bag. (부정문으로) → _____

2. Steve played baseball. (의문문으로) → _____

Practice 1 　다음 문장을 부정문으로 고치시오.

1. He has a good friend. → _____
2. Dora slept very well. → _____
3. Robert had an old lamp. → _____
4. My cousin carried the box. → _____
5. We listened to music. → _____
6. Judy made pizza for dinner. → _____
7. She teaches art at school. → _____

Practice 2 　다음 문장의 밑줄 친 부분을 바르게 고치시오.

1. <u>Do your sister has</u> breakfast? → _____
2. <u>Does you like</u> fruit and vegetables? → _____
3. <u>Does they play</u> computer games? → _____
4. <u>Do Jessica got</u> up early yesterday? → _____
5. <u>Do Charles washes</u> his hair every day? → _____
6. <u>Do they goes</u> to church every Sunday? → _____
7. <u>Does you enjoy</u> many sports then? → _____

Practice 3 　다음 질문에 알맞은 대답을 쓰시오.

1. Did you hurt your finger? – Yes, _____ _____ .
2. Does Tom love Sarah? – Yes, _____ _____ .
3. Does Eric have two daughters? – _____ , _____ doesn't.
4. Did she buy a desk? – No, _____ _____ .
5. Did Jerry leave New York? – _____ , _____ did.
6. Do Mark and his sister go jogging? – Yes, _____ _____ .
7. Did he see a strange man? – _____ , _____ didn't.

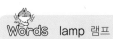 **Words** lamp 램프　cousin 사촌　vegetable 야채　church 교회　finger 손가락　strange 이상한

27

Review Test 1

A. 다음 밑줄 친 부분을 바르게 고치시오.

1. Brian and his wife <u>has</u> many dogs.

2. I <u>not</u> know the answer yesterday.

3. Mr. Jason <u>run</u> to the market every day.

4. <u>Do</u> your sister work at the airport?

B. 다음 괄호 안의 단어를 알맞은 형태로 바꿔 빈칸에 쓰시오.

1. He _____ many books last night. (read)

2. Sarah _____ new glasses yesterday. (buy)

3. A prince _____ a princess a long time ago. (love)

4. My family _____ dinner at a restaurant yesterday. (eat)

5. My sister _____ to the movies last week. (go)

C. 다음 괄호 안의 지시대로 문장을 바꿔 쓰시오.

1. Kevin has a nice bike. (부정문으로)

   → _____

2. You found an old coin on the street. (의문문으로)

   → _____

3. Do you cook well? (주어를 your mother로)

   → _____

D. 다음 우리말과 같도록 주어진 단어를 이용하여 문장을 쓰시오.

1. 그 고양이는 쥐 한 마리를 잡았다. (catch)

   → _____

2. Sam과 그의 아들은 벤치에 앉았다. (sit)

   → _____

3. 너희들은 그 게임에 졌니? (lose)

   → _____

4. 우리는 그때 노래를 부르지 않았다. (sing)

   → _____

Words

A. many 많은
market 시장
airport 공항

B. glasses 안경
prince 왕자
princess 공주

C. coin 동전
street 거리
cook 요리하다

D. catch 잡다
son 아들
lose 지다, 잃다

1. 다음 동사의 3인칭 단수형이 잘못 짝지어진 것은?
   ① enjoy – enjoys   ② go – goes
   ③ fix – fixs   ④ have – has
   ⑤ cry – cries

2. 다음 문장의 빈칸에 알맞은 것은?

   _____ likes vegetables.

   ① The students   ② Jenny
   ③ We   ④ You
   ⑤ She and I

3. 다음 대화의 빈칸에 공통으로 알맞은 것은?

   A: _____ you sleep well last night?
   B: Yes, I _____.

   ① do   ② does
   ③ did   ④ don't
   ⑤ didn't

4. 다음 빈칸에 들어갈 알맞은 동사는?

   He _____ to school two hours ago.

   ① go   ② goes
   ③ went   ④ is
   ⑤ was

5. 다음 빈칸에 have를 쓸 수 없는 것은?
   ① I _____ a pet.
   ② They _____ an old computer.
   ③ Janet _____ a big garden.
   ④ Mark and his friend _____ many books.
   ⑤ We _____ dinner around seven o'clock.

6. 다음 문장을 〈보기〉와 같이 바꿔 쓰시오.

   〈보기〉 He makes many cookies.
         → Does he make many cookies?

   He bought a new camera.
   → _____

7. 다음 중 밑줄 친 동사의 과거형이 잘못된 것은?
   ① My dad made spaghetti.
   ② Tom readed books in the library.
   ③ I lost my bag on the subway.
   ④ Mr. Johnson put his coat on the sofa.
   ⑤ She sang a song loudly.

8. 다음 우리말과 같은 뜻이 되도록 빈칸에 알맞은 것은?

   나는 어제 TV를 보지 않았다.
   → I _____ TV yesterday.

   ① don't watch   ② doesn't watch
   ③ didn't watched   ④ didn't watch
   ⑤ watched not

9. 다음 빈칸에 Do가 올 수 <u>없는</u> 것은?

① _____ you have a good time?

② _____ you read these books?

③ _____ you get up early?

④ _____ you clean your house?

⑤ _____ you buy a hat yesterday?

10. 다음 빈칸에 들어갈 말이 바르게 짝지어진 것은?

> A: Did you _____ at home then?
> B: No, I didn't. I _____ Kate.

① stay – meet   ② stay – met

③ stayed – meet   ④ stayed – met

⑤ stays – met

11. 다음 중 어법상 <u>어색한</u> 것은?

① I don't enjoy the movies.

② My mother doesn't drink coffee.

③ They doesn't play soccer.

④ Jack doesn't work at a bank.

⑤ Many people don't like him.

12. 다음 중 의문문이 자연스러운 것은?

① Are you get up late?

② Does Mark has lunch?

③ Does she come here on time?

④ Does Amy studies history?

⑤ Do they carries their boxes?

13. 다음 질문에 대한 알맞은 대답은?

> Does Ashley know the way?

① Yes, she is.   ② No, I don't.

③ No, she doesn't. ④ Yes, she do.

⑤ No, she does.

14. 다음 중 밑줄 친 부분이 바르지 <u>않은</u> 것은?

① She <u>washes</u> the dishes.

② The leaves <u>turns</u> red.

③ The baby <u>cries</u> loudly.

④ It <u>rains</u> a lot in summer.

⑤ He often <u>helps</u> the old man.

15. 다음 빈칸에 들어갈 말로 <u>어색한</u> 것은?

> She _____ Judy in the park yesterday.

① saw   ② met

③ plays with   ④ talked with

⑤ waited for

16. 다음 빈칸에 공통으로 알맞은 말은?

> · He _____ a watch last month.
> · They _____ the game then.

① wrote   ② were

③ won   ④ brought

⑤ lost

명사란 무엇인가?

사람이나 동물, 사물, 장소 등 세상에 있는 모든 것들의 이름을
나타내는 말을 명사라고 한다. 명사는 셀 수 있는 명사와 셀 수
없는 명사가 있는데, 셀 수 있는 명사가 둘 이상일 경우에는 명
사의 복수형으로 나타낸다.

관사란 무엇인가?

관사는 명사 앞에 붙어서 명사의 의미를 명확히 해주는데, 명사
앞에 어떤 관사가 오느냐에 따라서 그 의미가 달라진다. 가리키
는 대상(명사)이 정해져 있을 때는 the를 쓰고, 그 대상(명사)이
정해져 있지 않을 때는 a나 an을 쓴다.

Chapter 3. 명사와 관사

08 명사의 단수와 복수

1. 명사의 단수와 복수

· 명사는 사람이나 사물, 장소 등의 이름을 나타내는 말로 하나는 단수, 둘 이상은 복수라고 한다.

I have a **pencil**. He has three **pencils**. 나는 연필이 1개 있다. 그는 연필이 3개 있다.

* 셀 수 있는 명사는 복수형을 만들 수 있지만, 셀 수 없는 명사는 복수형을 만들 수 없다.

I drink **milk** every morning. 나는 매일 아침에 우유를 마신다.

* 셀 수 없는 명사에는 고유명사, 물질명사, 추상명사가 있다.

1. 고유명사(사람, 지역, 나라 이름) – Amy, Carol, Seoul, Korea 등(첫 글자는 항상 대문자로 표기)
2. 물질명사(형태가 없는 기체, 액체, 고체, 가루 등) – sugar, water, air, money, milk 등
3. 추상명사(추상적인 개념, 감정) – love, beauty, peace, hope, health, luck 등

> **Check 1** 셀 수 있는 명사에는 ○표, 셀 수 없는 명사에는 ×표 하시오.
>
> 1. house (   )   2. peace (   )
> 3. rain   (   )   4. Japan (   )

2. 명사의 복수형 : 규칙 변화

· 명사의 복수형 만드는 방법

대부분의 명사	명사+-s	book → books, girl → girls, lion → lions
-o, -x, -s(s), -sh, -ch 로 끝나는 명사	명사+-es	tomato → tomatoes, box → boxes, bus → buses, dish → dishes, bench → benches 예외) pianos, photos
「자음+y」로 끝나는 명사	-y를 i로 고치고 +-es	baby → babies, lady → ladies, candy → candies
「모음+y」로 끝나는 명사	명사+-s	toy → toys, boy → boys, tray → trays
-f, -fe로 끝나는 명사	-f, -fe를 v로 고치고+-es	knife → knives, leaf → leaves, wife → wives 예외) roofs

3. 명사의 복수형 : 불규칙 변화

단수형 ≠ 복수형	man → men, woman → women, tooth → teeth, foot → feet, child → children, mouse → mice, goose → geese, ox → oxen
단수형 = 복수형	sheep → sheep, fish → fish, deer → deer

> **Check 2** 다음 명사의 복수형을 쓰시오.
>
> 1. child → _____   2. leaf → _____
> 3. city   → _____   4. foot → _____

4. 물질명사의 수량표현

· 주로 단위나 용기 등을 사용해서 나타내고 복수형은 단위나 용기를 나타내는 말에 복수형을 쓴다.

a cup of (~ 1잔)	a cup of coffee → two cups of coffee
a glass of (~ 1잔)	a glass of water → three glasses of water
a bottle of (~ 1병)	a bottle of juice → four bottles of juice
a piece of (~ 1조각)	a piece of cake[paper] → two pieces of cake[paper]

* 항상 복수형을 쓰는 명사(pants, shoes, socks, scissors)는 a pair of를 써서 수를 나타낸다.

a pair of pants → two pairs of pants

Practice 1 — 다음 단어의 복수형을 쓰시오.

1. umbrella → _____
2. bus → _____
3. knife → _____
4. potato → _____
5. hat → _____
6. roof → _____
7. man → _____
8. sheep → _____
9. baby → _____
10. woman → _____
11. dish → _____
12. ox → _____
13. toy → _____
14. teacher → _____

Practice 2 — 다음 주어진 단어를 알맞은 형태로 바꿔 쓰시오.

1. My brother has only two _____. (tooth)
2. Nick has a lot of _____. (photo)
3. Look at those _____. (fish)
4. Karen bought four _____. (tomato)
5. He and his wife traveled many _____. (country)
6. Those _____ are very beautiful. (house)
7. Two old _____ sat on the bench. (lady)

Practice 3 — 다음 밑줄 친 부분을 바르게 고치시오.

1. The girl bought two book. → _____
2. It's cold. Put on your glove. → _____
3. I drink four cups of waters every day. → _____
4. Jenny wants two pair of scissors. → _____
5. There are five pianoes in this room. → _____
6. Emily ate two piece of cake. → _____
7. Johnson has four puppys. → _____

Words roof 지붕   photo 사진   travel 여행하다   lady 숙녀   put on 입다   scissors 가위   puppy 강아지

09 부정관사와 정관사

1. 부정관사 a, an

· 부정관사 a, an은 '하나'라는 뜻으로 정해지지 않은 것을 나타낼 때 사용하며 셀 수 있는 명사 앞에 쓴다. 명사의 첫소리가 자음이면 a, 모음이면 an을 쓴다.

막연한 하나	He is **a** teacher. She is **an** actress.
하나의	I have **a** robot. I eat **an** apple and bread for lunch.
매 ~, ~마다	I go to church once **a** week.

· 부정관사와 명사 사이에 형용사가 오면 형용사의 첫소리에 따라 a나 an을 쓴다.

It's **an** interesting story. 그것은 재미있는 이야기이다.

It's **a** yellow umbrella. 그것은 노란색 우산이다.

Check 1 다음 괄호 안에서 알맞은 것을 고르시오.

1. There is (a / an) album in the drawer.

2. She bought (a / an) fresh orange.

3. I need (a / an) eraser.

---

2. 정관사 the

· 정관사 the는 특정한 것을 가리키며 명사의 종류나 단수, 복수에 관계없이 쓸 수 있다.

앞에 나온 명사를 다시 말할 때	I have a hamster. **The** hamster is very cute.
서로 알고 있는 것을 가리킬 때	Open **the** window, please.
수식어로 의미가 분명할 때	**The** bag on the table is red.
세상에 하나뿐인 것과 방위를 가리킬 때	**The** moon moves around **the** earth. ＊world, sea, sky, ground 앞에도 the를 쓴다.
악기 이름 앞에	I play **the** piano.

3. 관사를 쓰지 않는 경우

· 식사, 운동, 과목 등의 앞에는 관사를 쓰지 않는다.

식사, 운동 경기 앞에	I have **dinner** at seven p.m. She plays **tennis** with her friends.
과목명 앞에	I like **math** and **science**.
「by+교통수단」	I go to the museum **by bus**.
건물이 본래 목적으로 쓰일 때	Mike **goes to school** at eight a.m. ＊go to church, after school, go to bed

---

Check 2 다음 빈칸에 the가 필요하면 ○표, 필요 없으면 ×표 하시오.

1. I don't have _____ breakfast.

2. He plays _____ violin every day.

3. Close _____ door, please.

34

다음 빈칸에 a, an, the 중 알맞은 것을 쓰시오.

1. My uncle is _____ actor.
2. _____ earth is round.
3. She has _____ pretty daughter.
4. Sarah bought _____ new umbrella.
5. He plays _____ guitar on the stage.
6. The sun rises in _____ east.
7. Children play soccer for _____ hour.

다음 빈칸에 the가 필요하면 the를 쓰고, 필요 없으면 ×표 하시오.

1. My sons play _____ baseball well.
2. We go to _____ church on Sundays.
3. Open _____ door, please.
4. Susie has _____ breakfast at 7:00.
5. They go to school by _____ bus.
6. Pass me _____ salt, please.
7. She plays _____ cello very well.

다음 괄호 안에서 필요한 것을 골라 문장을 완성하시오.

1. 나는 새 휴대전화가 필요하다. (new, a, an, cell phone)
   → I need _____.

2. 그들은 멋진 정원을 보았다. (garden, nice, a, an)
   → They saw _____.

3. Vicky는 버스로 그녀의 삼촌을 방문했다. (by, a, the, bus)
   → Vicky visited her uncle _____.

4. 그는 하루에 2시간 영어를 공부한다. (two, a, the, day, hours)
   → He studies English for _____.

5. 하늘에 많은 별들이 있다. (sky, a, the, in)
   → There are many stars _____.

6. 나의 여동생은 파란색 모자를 쓰고 있다. (blue, a, an, hat)
   → My sister is wearing _____.

Words actor 배우 round 둥근 stage 무대 salt 소금 cello 첼로 garden 정원 visit 방문하다 wear 입다

Review Test 1

A. 다음 명사의 복수형을 쓰고, 복수형으로 쓸 수 없는 명사는 ×표 하시오.

1. city → _____
2. box → _____
3. health → _____
4. man → _____
5. Japan → _____
6. wolf → _____
7. deer → _____
8. boy → _____
9. juice → _____
10. foot → _____

B. 다음 괄호 안에서 알맞은 것을 고르시오.

1. There is (a / an) MP3 player in the bag.
2. He takes Chinese classes twice (a / the) week.
3. It's hot. Open (a / the) window, please.
4. (A / The) moon shines in (a / the / ×) sky.
5. My favorite subject is (a / the / ×) science.

C. 다음 밑줄 친 부분을 바르게 고치시오.

1. A happiness is around us. → _____
2. There are many bus on the street. → _____
3. They need two pieces of cheeses. → _____
4. Jake saw some leafs on the ground. → _____

D. 다음 우리말과 같도록 괄호 안의 단어를 이용하여 빈칸에 쓰시오.

1. Sam과 나는 방과 후에 축구를 한다. (after)
   → Sam and I play soccer _____.

2. 나는 매일 아침 우유 한 잔을 마신다. (a glass of)
   → I drink _____ every morning.

3. 그들은 일요일마다 함께 저녁 식사를 한다. (have)
   → They _____ together every Sunday.

4. 태양은 서쪽으로 진다. (west)
   → The sun sets in _____.

Words

A. health 건강
   wolf 늑대
   deer 사슴

B. twice 두 번
   shine 빛나다
   subject 과목

C. happiness 행복
   need 필요하다
   cheese 치즈
   leaf 나뭇잎

D. after ~ 후에
   drink 마시다
   together 함께
   west 서쪽

1. 다음 중 단수와 복수가 잘못 짝지어진 것은?

   ① dress – dresses
   ② photo – photoes
   ③ woman – women
   ④ tooth – teeth
   ⑤ sheep – sheep

2. 다음 중 명사의 복수형 만드는 방법이 다른 것은?

   ① wife   ② roof
   ③ leaf   ④ thief
   ⑤ knife

3. 다음 중 a 또는 an의 쓰임이 올바른 것은?

   ① a umbrella
   ② a old lady
   ③ an fresh orange
   ④ an empty bottle
   ⑤ a hour

4. 다음 중 명사의 복수형이 잘못된 것은?

   ① My aunt has two babies.
   ② The apples are green.
   ③ She washes the dishes.
   ④ There are ten sheepes.
   ⑤ She has many deer.

[5–6] 다음 중 어법상 어색한 것을 고르시오.

5. ① Kelly is in the bedroom.
   ② Brad has an old camera.
   ③ I wash the dishes once the week.
   ④ The shoes on the box are not mine.
   ⑤ The moon doesn't have air.

6. ① She is not a famous artist.
   ② His mother works at a bank.
   ③ I'm thirsty. Give me some water.
   ④ The children drink milks every day.
   ⑤ We have three meals a day.

7. 다음 빈칸에 알맞지 않은 것은?

   There are two _____ in the room.

   ① tomatoes   ② eggs
   ③ children   ④ bags
   ⑤ table

8. 다음 중 빈칸에 a 또는 an을 쓸 수 없는 것은?

   ① I have _____ apple.
   ② He is _____ great artist.
   ③ Sarah plays _____ piano every day.
   ④ We bought _____ new computer.
   ⑤ They saw _____ ostrich on the farm.

[9–10] 다음 밑줄 친 부분이 어색한 것을 고르시오.

9. ① I have two sons.
   ② Those are glasses.
   ③ There are churchs there.
   ④ She has four puppies.
   ⑤ The potatoes are big.

10. ① Men have ten fingers.
    ② We drink a coffee.
    ③ They have a cat.
    ④ She likes candies.
    ⑤ He has many dolls.

11. 다음 중 빈칸에 부정관사를 쓸 수 없는 것은?
    ① This is _____ bike.
    ② We are _____ artists.
    ③ There is _____ apple.
    ④ He has _____ album.
    ⑤ She is _____ dentist.

12. 다음 빈칸에 a가 필요한 것은?
    ① I have _____ lunch at noon.
    ② Please give me _____ water.
    ③ He needs _____ some bread.
    ④ We like _____ math very much.
    ⑤ This is _____ book.

13. 다음 중 빈칸에 들어갈 말이 나머지와 다른 것은?
    ① _____ earth is round.
    ② We can't see _____ moon tonight.
    ③ I can play _____ guitar well.
    ④ There is an eagle in _____ sky.
    ⑤ Ann has _____ doll. The doll is cute.

14. 다음 빈칸에 들어갈 말이 순서대로 짝지어진 것은?

    I ate _____ apple for breakfast.
    _____ apple was delicious.

    ① an – The   ② an – An
    ③ the – An   ④ a – The
    ⑤ the – A

15. 다음 중 빈칸에 관사가 필요 없는 것은?
    ① I want to be _____ musician.
    ② The train goes to _____ south.
    ③ I'm looking for _____ shirt.
    ④ Take this medicine three times _____ day.
    ⑤ We don't go to _____ school on Sundays.

16. 다음 ①~⑤ 중 the가 들어갈 알맞은 곳은?

    I was busy (①) yesterday. I played (②) violin for (③) two hours and had (④) lunch with my cousin. After lunch, I played (⑤) basketball with Jim.

진행시제란 무엇인가?
진행시제는 현재 또는 과거의 한 시점에서 진행 중인 동작을 나타내며 '～하는 중이(었)다, ～하고 있(었)다'의 뜻이다.

미래시제란 무엇인가?
현재의 일은 현재시제로 나타내고 과거의 일은 과거시제로 나타내는 것처럼 미래시제는 앞으로 일어날 일이나 계획, 의지를 나타낼 때 사용한다. 미래시제는 조동사 will이나 be going to를 동사 앞에 붙여서 만들며 '～일 것이다', '～할 것이다'라는 뜻이다.

Chapter 4. 동사의 시제

10 현재시제와 과거시제

1. 현재시제

· 현재의 상태나 직업을 나타낸다.

I **am** tired and sleepy. 나는 피곤하고 졸리다.

He **works** for a bank. 그는 은행에서 일한다.

· 일상적인 습관이나 반복적인 동작을 나타낸다.

She **walks** her dog every evening. 그녀는 매일 저녁 그녀의 개를 산책시킨다.

I **get** up at 7:00 every morning. 나는 매일 아침 7시에 일어난다.

· 일반적인 사실이나 불변의 진리를 나타낸다.

We **have** four seasons in Korea. 한국에는 사계절이 있다.

The moon **moves** around the earth. 달은 지구 주위를 돈다.

Water **freezes** at 0℃ and **boils** at 100℃. 물은 0℃에서 얼고 100℃에서 끓는다.

* 시제 : 시간의 흐름을 현재, 과거, 미래와 같이 구분하는 것을 말한다. 현재는 지금 일어나는 일을, 과거는 지나간 일을, 미래는 앞으로 일어날 일을 말한다.

Check 1 다음 괄호 안에서 알맞은 것을 고르시오.

1. I (play / played) soccer every Sunday.

2. It (is / was) hot in summer.

3. My mother (have / has) black hair.

---

2. 과거시제

· 과거 한 시점의 동작이나 상태를 나타내며 주로 과거를 나타내는 부사(구)와 함께 쓴다.

They **went** to the museum yesterday. 그들은 어제 박물관에 갔다.

I **was** an elementary school student last year. 나는 작년에 초등학생이었다.

· 역사적 사실은 항상 과거시제로 나타낸다.

Columbus **discovered** America in 1492. Columbus는 1492년에 아메리카를 발견했다.

Thomas Edison **invented** the light bulb. Thomas Edison은 전구를 발명했다.

* 과거를 나타내는 부사(구)에는 yesterday, last, ago, then, at that time 등이 있다.

Check 2 다음 괄호 안의 단어를 알맞은 형태로 바꿔 쓰시오.

1. It _____ cool last Sunday. (is)

2. We _____ hiking yesterday. (go)

3. He _____ a bike at that time. (ride)

Practice 1　다음 밑줄 친 부분을 바르게 고치시오.

1. She <u>reads</u> a book a few minutes ago.　→ _____

2. I <u>got</u> up 6:00 every morning.　→ _____

3. He <u>watches</u> a movie yesterday.　→ _____

4. My mother <u>went</u> to church on Sundays.　→ _____

5. I <u>hear</u> the strange sound last night.　→ _____

6. They <u>plant</u> many flowers last Monday.　→ _____

7. Ryan <u>drank</u> coffee every morning.　→ _____

Practice 2　다음 괄호 안의 단어를 알맞은 형태로 바꿔 쓰시오.

1. 그녀는 갈색의 머리를 가지고 있다. (have)　→ She _____ brown hair.

2. Julie는 어제 그 가방을 잃어버렸다. (lose)　→ Julie _____ the bag yesterday.

3. 그는 잠자기 전에 양치질을 한다. (brush)　→ He _____ his teeth before bed.

4. 가을에는 나뭇잎이 떨어진다. (fall)　→ The leaves _____ in autumn.

5. 나는 오늘 아침에 음악을 들었다. (listen)　→ I _____ to music this morning.

6. 그는 방학 동안 일본에 있었다. (stay)　→ He _____ in Japan during vacation.

7. 지구는 태양 주위를 돈다. (go)　→ The earth _____ around the sun.

Practice 3　다음 〈보기〉에서 알맞은 동사를 골라 빈칸에 쓰시오.

〈보기〉 had　　go　　is　　has　　sang　　was　　baked

1. A giraffe _____ a long neck.

2. They _____ fun at the concert last weekend.

3. It _____ very hot and humid in August.

4. She _____ very sick yesterday.

5. I _____ to bed at 10:00 every day.

6. My sister and I _____ and danced together last night.

7. Laura _____ the cookies about two hours ago.

Words　strange 이상한　sound 소리　plant 심다　autumn 가을　earth 지구　giraffe 기린　humid 습한, 축축한

Unit 11 진행시제의 쓰임과 형태

1. 진행시제

· 특정 시점에서 진행 중인 동작을 나타내며 「be동사+동사원형-ing」의 형태로 쓴다.

He **is going** to school. 그는 학교에 가고 있다.

· 동사의 -ing형 만드는 방법

대부분의 동사	동사원형+-ing	eat → eating, read → reading
-e로 끝나는 동사	e를 빼고+-ing	dance → dancing, make → making
「단모음+단자음」으로 끝나는 1음절 동사	자음을 한 번 더 쓰고 +-ing	run → running, swim → swimming
-ie로 끝나는 동사	ie를 y로 고치고+-ing	lie → lying, tie → tying

* 소유나 상태를 나타내는 동사인 have, know, love, hate, want 등은 진행시제로 쓸 수 없다. 단, have 가 '먹다, (시간을) 보내다'의 의미로 쓰일 때는 진행시제로 쓸 수 있다.

She is having dinner. (O)　　We are having a good time. (O)

Check 1 다음 일반동사의 -ing형을 쓰시오.

1. cut　→ ＿＿＿＿＿＿＿
2. clean　→ ＿＿＿＿＿＿＿
3. die　→ ＿＿＿＿＿＿＿
4. bake　→ ＿＿＿＿＿＿＿

---

2. 현재진행형, 과거진행형

· 현재의 진행 중인 동작은 현재진행형으로 나타내고 과거의 진행 중인 동작은 과거진행형으로 나타낸다.

	현재진행형	과거진행형
형태	am, are, is+동사원형-ing	was, were+동사원형-ing
의미	~하는 중이다, ~하고 있다 (현재 진행 중인 동작)	~하는 중이었다, ~하고 있었다 (과거의 한 시점에서 진행 중인 동작)
예문	I **am studying** now. She **is cooking** in the kitchen.	I **was swimming** at that time. They **were playing** computer games.

---

3. 진행시제의 부정문과 의문문

· 진행시제의 부정문과 의문문은 be동사의 부정문, 의문문 만드는 방법과 같다.

	부정문	의문문
형태	주어+be동사+not+동사원형-ing ~.	Be동사+주어+동사원형-ing ~? - Yes, 주어+be동사. / 　No, 주어+be동사+not.
예문	I am **not listening** to music. We were **not talking** about her.	**Are** you **going** to the hospital? - Yes, I am. / No, I'm not. **Was** she **watching** TV yesterday? - Yes, she was. / No, she wasn't.

Check 2 다음 괄호 안의 단어를 알맞은 형태로 바꿔 쓰시오.

1. Linda was not ＿＿＿＿＿＿＿ at that time. (draw)
2. I'm ＿＿＿＿＿＿＿ a house now. (build)

Practice 1 | 다음 괄호 안의 동사를 이용해 현재진행형 문장을 완성하시오.

1. Peter _____ his hands. (wash)

2. My father _____ tea in the garden. (drink)

3. I _____ the dishes in the kitchen. (do)

4. Ted _____ in the park now. (read)

5. They _____ some food. (cook)

6. Vicky and Philip _____ for Judy. (wait)

7. Mr. Brown _____ with his son. (play)

Practice 2 | 다음 문장의 시제에 유의하여 진행형 문장으로 바꿔 쓰시오.

1. He wrote a letter to his friend.   → _____

2. The wind blows hard today.   → _____

3. I draw a picture in the park.   → _____

4. The boy ran fast to the store.   → _____

5. My dad has dinner at home.   → _____

6. She made a cake for Peter.   → _____

7. They sell hats and bags there.   → _____

Practice 3 | 다음 문장을 괄호 안의 지시대로 바꾸시오.

1. He is inventing something. (부정문으로)   → _____

2. Eagles were flying away. (의문문으로)   → _____

3. Ted washed the car. (진행형으로)   → _____

4. Kids were playing soccer. (부정문으로)   → _____

5. A dog was barking then. (부정문으로)   → _____

6. Babies slept on the bed. (진행형으로)   → _____

7. Carol collects foreign coins. (진행형으로)   → _____

Words garden 정원 blow 불다 sell 팔다 invent 발명하다 bark 짖다 collect 모으다 foreign 외국의

12 미래시제(will, be going to)

1. 미래시제

· 미래의 일이나 의지, 예정된 계획을 나타내며 will 또는 be going to를 써서 나타낸다.

It **will** be sunny tomorrow. 내일은 맑게 갤 것이다.

He **is going to** read the books. 그는 그 책들을 읽을 것이다.

2. will

· will은 '~할 것이다, ~일 것이다'라는 뜻으로 미래에 일어날 일에 대한 예측이나 계획, 또는 의지를 나타낸다.

긍정문	주어+will+동사원형 ~.	I **will** go to Paris next year.
부정문	주어+will not[won't]+동사원형 ~.	I **will not** go to Paris next year.
의문문	Will+주어+동사원형 ~? – Yes, 주어+will. / No, 주어+won't.	**Will** you go to Paris next year? – Yes, I will. / No, I won't.

＊ will not은 won't로 줄여서 사용할 수 있다.

＊ I will은 I'll로, You will은 You'll(He will은 He'll, She will은 She'll, …)로 줄여서 사용할 수 있다.

> **Check 1** 다음 괄호 안에서 알맞은 것을 고르시오.
>
> 1. David will (is / be) at home this Sunday.
> 2. I (will not / not will) eat out in the evening.
> 3. Will she (visit / visits) her grandparents?

3. be going to

· be going to는 '~할 것이다, ~일 것이다'라는 뜻으로 가까운 미래의 일이나 예정된 계획을 나타낸다.

긍정문	주어+be동사+going to+동사원형 ~.	She **is going to** see a movie.
부정문	주어+be동사+not going to+동사원형 ~.	She **is not going** to see a movie.
의문문	Be동사+주어+going to+동사원형 ~? – Yes, 주어+be동사. / No, 주어+be동사+not.	Is she **going to** see a movie? – Yes, she is. / No, she isn't.

＊ will은 be going to로 바꾸어 쓸 수 있는데, 객관적인 사실은 be going to로 바꿀 수 없다.

I will be fourteen years old next year. (will → am going to ×)

＊ be going to+동사원형은 미래시제를 나타내고 be going to+장소는 진행형을 나타낸다.

> **Check 2** 다음 괄호 안에서 알맞은 것을 고르시오.
>
> 1. She is (will / going to) play badminton.
> 2. (Is / Are) the boys going to the museum?
> 3. He (won't / is not going) to wear the cap.

다음 밑줄 친 부분을 바르게 고치시오.

1. I'm <u>going to seeing</u> a dentist. → _____

2. She <u>won't stays</u> in Jeju this week. → _____

3. He <u>wills arrive</u> at the airport. → _____

4. You <u>is going to</u> watch a movie. → _____

5. Ron <u>will passes</u> the exam. → _____

6. Peter <u>is going not</u> to save the money. → _____

7. Is she going <u>to has</u> a party soon? → _____

Practice 2 다음 괄호 안의 단어를 배열하여 문장을 완성하시오.

1. (is, play, he, not, going, to, tennis) → _____

2. (be, very, cool, this autumn, will) → _____

3. (sneakers, buy, new, she, will) → _____

4. (a truck, will, my father, drive, ?) → _____

5. (is, take a rest, to, she, going) → _____

6. (not, drink, I, going, coffee, am, to) → _____

7. (be, won't, they, tomorrow, busy) → _____

Practice 3 다음 대화의 빈칸에 알맞은 말을 쓰시오.

1. _____ she come home early? – Yes, she will.

2. _____ Harry going to go shopping? – _____, he is.

3. Is the game _____ to start soon? – Yes, _____ _____.

4. _____ Jordan solve the problem? – _____, _____ will.

5. Will they move to Seoul next year? – _____, _____ won't.

6. Are you going to take piano lessons? – No, _____ _____.

7. Will Anna have a party tomorrow? – _____, _____ won't.

Words arrive 도착하다   pass 합격하다   truck 트럭   rest 휴식   solve 풀다   problem 문제   move 이사하다

A. 다음 빈칸에 알맞은 말을 〈보기〉에서 골라 문장에 맞게 고쳐 쓰시오.

〈보기〉 visit   be   invite   read

1. He _____ me to the party last night.
2. Cindy _____ four books every month.
3. Tokyo _____ the capital of Japan.
4. The singer _____ Busan last weekend.

B. 문장의 밑줄 친 부분을 어법에 맞게 고치시오.

1. It <u>snows</u> yesterday and it rains today.   → _____
2. <u>Was</u> he drawing the picture now?   → _____
3. He <u>is</u> looking for his purse last night.   → _____
4. My aunt will <u>travels</u> around the world.   → _____

C. 다음 우리말과 같도록 빈칸에 알맞은 말을 쓰시오.

1. 그녀는 너에게 전화할 것이다. (call)
   → She _____ _____ you.

2. 그는 그의 여동생을 돌보지 않고 있었다. (be)
   → He _____ _____ taking care of his sister.

3. 그들은 벤치에 앉아 있다. (sit)
   → They _____ _____ on the bench.

4. Vicky는 그녀의 친구를 기다리고 있는 중이니? (wait)
   → _____ Vicky _____ for her friend?

D. 다음 괄호 안의 지시대로 문장을 바꿔 쓰시오.

1. The baby cried on the bed. (진행형으로)
   → _____

2. I'm going to write a letter tonight. (부정문으로)
   → _____

3. They are going to learn Chinese. (의문문으로)
   → _____

4. He went hiking with his family. (will, 미래시제로)
   → _____

Words

A. invite 초대하다
   capital 수도
   weekend 주말

B. purse 지갑
   travel 여행하다

C. call 부르다, 전화하다
   wait 기다리다

D. tonight 오늘 밤에
   learn 배우다
   hiking 하이킹

1. 다음 동사와 -ing형이 <u>잘못된</u> 것은?

① ride – riding
② help – helping
③ shop – shopping
④ tie – tying
⑤ fly – fling

2. 다음 빈칸에 알맞은 것은?

Columbus _____ America in 1492.

① discover
② discovers
③ is discovering
④ discovered
⑤ discovering

3. 다음 문장을 진행형으로 바르게 바꾼 것은?

My brother makes a big kite.

① My brother making a big kite.
② My brother is making a big kite.
③ My brother are making a big kite.
④ My brother am making a big kite.
⑤ My brother does making a big kite.

4. 다음 중 어법상 <u>어색한</u> 것은?

① I went to bed early last night.
② I take a shower every morning.
③ My mother will be sleepy now.
④ They are taking pictures.
⑤ We have lots of rain in summer.

5. 다음 밑줄 친 부분과 바꿔 쓸 수 있는 것은?

I <u>will</u> go to the zoo tomorrow.

① am going to
② is going to
③ are going to
④ was going to
⑤ were going to

6. 다음 밑줄 친 부분의 쓰임이 <u>잘못된</u> 것은?

① I'm <u>having</u> dinner.
② Today <u>is</u> my birthday.
③ The sun <u>rose</u> in the east.
④ She <u>put</u> her gloves on the desk.
⑤ They are going to <u>meet</u> their aunt.

7. 다음 빈칸에 공통으로 알맞은 것은?

· I am _____ to the bookstore.
· He is not _____ to buy a car.

① go
② going
③ went
④ will
⑤ do

8. 다음 빈칸에 들어갈 말이 순서대로 바르게 짝지어 진 것은?

· She _____ coffee every morning.
· He _____ coffee last night.

① drinks – drinks
② drank – drinks
③ drinks – drank
④ drink – drank
⑤ drank – drank

9. 다음 중 내용상 빈칸에 알맞은 것은?

> I'm very tired. So I _____ the violin this afternoon.

① will practice   ② practiced

③ wasn't practicing   ④ won't practice

⑤ practice soon

10. 다음 밑줄 친 부분의 쓰임이 나머지와 다른 것은?

① We're <u>going to</u> church now.

② I'm <u>going to</u> buy some carrots.

③ They're <u>going to</u> ride bikes.

④ He's <u>going to</u> have a party.

⑤ She's <u>going to</u> be busy tomorrow.

[11-12] 다음 중 자연스러운 문장을 고르시오.

11. ① Is she ride a bicycle?

② Is it raining in London?

③ Do you washing a car?

④ She am writing a letter now.

⑤ He doesn't playing tennis.

12. ① He will play soccer tomorrow.

② My mom wills go to the market.

③ She will passes the exam soon.

④ Will he comes back next weekend?

⑤ Matt are going to watch a movie.

13. 다음 중 과거를 나타나는 말이 아닌 것은?

① then   ② yesterday

③ last month   ④ a few days ago

⑤ tomorrow

14. 다음 대화의 빈칸에 알맞은 대답은?

> A: Is she cooking in the kitchen?
> B: _____ She is making salad.

① Yes, she was.   ② Yes, she is.

③ Yes, she does.   ④ No, she wasn't.

⑤ No, she isn't.

15. 다음 빈칸에 들어갈 말이 나머지와 다른 것은?

① _____ she going to take a rest?

② _____ he sleeping on the bed now?

③ _____ Peter your friend?

④ _____ your dog sleeping last night?

⑤ _____ he going to listen to music?

16. 다음 중 의문문 문장이 바르지 않은 것은?

① Do they clean the street?

② Does Jonathan look happy?

③ Did she live in New York then?

④ Will you go on a picnic tomorrow?

⑤ Does he is going to do his homework?

의문사란 무엇인가?
'누가, 언제, 어디서, 무엇을, 어떻게, 왜'와 같이 의문이 나는 것을 물어보는 말을 의문사라고 한다. 의문사를 이용하여 의문문을 만들 때는 항상 의문사를 문장 맨 앞에 놓는다.

「How+형용사/부사」는 무슨 뜻인가?
how는 뒤에 형용사, 부사, many, much를 붙여서 상태나 수, 양 등의 질문을 만들 수 있다. 또한 키, 나이, 빈도, 거리, 길이 등 다양한 표현이 가능하다.

Chapter 5. 의문사

Unit 13. who, whose, what, which

Unit 14. when, where, why

Unit 15. how, how+형용사/부사

13 who, whose, what, which

1. who와 whose

· who는 '누구, 누가'라는 뜻으로 사람의 이름이나 사람과의 관계를 물을 때 쓴다.

Who is that girl? 저 소녀는 누구니?

– She is my sister. 그녀는 내 여동생이야.

Who broke the vase? 누가 꽃병을 깼니? (Who가 주어 역할 → 3인칭 단수 취급)

– Andy did. Andy가 그랬어.

· whose는 '누구의, 누구의 것'이라는 뜻으로 소유격이며 소유를 물을 때 쓴다. 대답은 소유격이나 소유대명사를 이용하여 답한다.

Whose book is this? 이것은 누구의 책이니? (Whose → 형용사)

– It's mine. 그것은 내 것이야.

Whose is that toy car? 저 장난감 자동차는 누구의 것이니? (Whose → 대명사)

– It's my brother's. 그것은 내 남동생 것이야.

* 의문사 의문문에 대한 대답은 Yes나 No로 하지 않고 의문사에 해당하는 말로 답한다.

> **Check 1** 다음 괄호 안에서 알맞은 것을 고르시오.
>
> 1. (Who / Whose) shoes are these?
> 2. (Who / Whose) is that kind woman?
> 3. (Who / Whose) lives in this house?

2. what과 which

· what은 '무엇, 어떤'이라는 뜻으로 사물의 이름이나 사람의 직업, 역할 등을 물을 때 쓴다.

What does your father do? 너의 아버지의 직업은 무엇이니?

– He is a cook. 그는 요리사야.

What sport do you like? 너는 어떤 운동을 좋아하니?

– I like soccer. 나는 축구를 좋아해.

· which는 '어느, 어느 것'이라는 뜻으로 정해진 대상 중에서 선택을 물을 때 쓴다.

Which do you want, coffee or tea? 너는 커피와 차 중에서 어느 것을 원하니?

– I want some coffee. 나는 커피를 좀 원해.

Which bag is yours? 어느 가방이 너의 것이니? (Which bag이 주어 역할)

– The blue bag is mine. 파란색 가방이 내 것이야.

> **Check 2** 다음 빈칸에 what이나 which 중 알맞은 것을 쓰시오.
>
> 1. _____ is his name? – He is James.
> 2. _____ car is yours, this or that? – That one.
> 3. _____ did you make there? – I made a model car.

Practice 1 다음 밑줄 친 부분을 바르게 고치시오.

1. <u>What</u> do you want, sugar or salt? → _____
2. <u>Whose</u> knows her address? → _____
3. <u>Who</u> dictionary is this? → _____
4. <u>What</u> do you like, apples or grapes? → _____
5. <u>Who</u> is your favorite subject? → _____
6. <u>Which</u> does she eat for lunch? → _____
7. <u>Whose</u> is your brother's job? → _____

Practice 2 다음 대화의 빈칸에 알맞은 의문사를 쓰시오.

1. _____ is the beautiful dress? – It's my sister's.
2. _____ sings songs in the hall? – Mary does.
3. _____ do you want? – I want a blue shirt.
4. _____ color do you like, green or blue?
5. _____ pants are those? – They are mine.
6. _____ do you want for lunch, pizza or sandwiches?
7. _____ is the handsome man? – He's my math teacher.

Practice 3 다음 우리말과 같도록 괄호 안의 단어를 바르게 배열하시오.

1. James는 무엇을 만들었니? (what, James, make, did)
   → _____

2. 저것은 누구의 빨간색 모자이니? (is, whose, red, that, cap)
   → _____

3. 누가 어제 Lucy를 만났니? (met, Lucy, yesterday, who)
   → _____

4. 네가 가장 좋아하는 배우는 누구니? (favorite, is, actor, who, your)
   → _____

5. 이 큰 보트는 누구의 것이니? (is, big, whose, boat, this)
   → _____

6. 너는 점심으로 무엇을 먹었니? (did, eat, for, what, you, lunch)
   → _____

7. 너는 봄과 가을 중 어느 계절을 좋아하니? (season, do, you, like, which, spring or fall)
   → _____

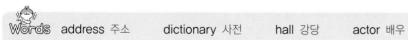

Words address 주소   dictionary 사전   hall 강당   actor 배우   season 계절   spring 봄

14 | when, where, why

1. when

· when은 '언제'라는 뜻으로 시간이나 날짜, 때를 물을 때 쓴다.

When is your birthday? 너의 생일은 언제니?

– It's November 24th. 11월 24일이야.

When do you have lunch? 너는 언제 점심을 먹니?

– I have lunch at 12:30. 12시 30분에 먹어.

＊when으로 시작하는 의문문의 대답은 시간의 전치사 at, in, on을 이용한다.

2. where

· where는 위치나 장소를 물을 때 쓴다.

Where is the bank? 그 은행은 어디에 있니?

– It's across the street. 그것은 길 건너편에 있어.

Where did you meet Bill? 너는 어디서 Bill을 만났니?

– I met him in the park. 나는 공원에서 그를 만났어.

＊where로 시작하는 의문문의 대답은 장소, 위치, 방향을 나타내는 전치사를 이용한다.

＊장소, 위치, 방향을 나타내는 전치사 : in, at, on, under, across, next to 등

Check 1 다음 우리말과 같은 뜻이 되도록 빈칸에 알맞은 말을 쓰시오.

1. ＿＿＿＿＿＿ is Children's Day? 어린이날은 언제니?

2. ＿＿＿＿＿＿ did you leave there? 너는 언제 거기를 떠났니?

3. ＿＿＿＿＿＿ is she going now? 그녀는 지금 어디 가니?

---

3. why

· why는 '왜'라는 뜻으로 이유나 원인을 물을 때 쓴다.

Why do you like this movie? 너는 왜 이 영화를 좋아하니?

– Because it's very interesting. 그것은 매우 재미있기 때문이야.

Why is he in a hurry? 그는 왜 서두르니?

– Because he is late for the meeting. 그는 그 모임에 늦었기 때문이야.

＊why로 시작하는 의문문의 대답은 because(~ 때문에)로 시작하는데 because는 생략할 수 있다.

Check 2 다음 대화의 빈칸에 알맞은 말을 쓰시오.

1. A: Why does she like Mike?

   B: ＿＿＿＿＿＿ he is very kind.

2. A: ＿＿＿＿＿＿ is she laughing?

   B: Because the movie is funny.

---

1. _____ do you go to school? (when, what)

2. _____ does the show start? (which, when)

3. _____ do the children go? (who, where)

4. _____ do you like summer most? (which, why)

5. _____ did you take a trip during vacation? (where, what)

6. _____ did Linda visit her grandparents? (whose, when)

7. _____ does she learn Spanish? (why, what)

1. 나의 신발은 어디에 있지? → _____ are my shoes?

2. Sally는 너에게 언제 전화했니? → _____ did Sally call you?

3. 저 소년들은 왜 신이 났니? → _____ are those boys excited?

4. 그 식당은 언제 문을 여니? → _____ does the restaurant open?

5. 사람들은 왜 Lily를 좋아하니? → _____ do people like Lily?

6. 그는 그의 열쇠를 어디에 놓았니? → _____ did he put his key?

7. 그 시험은 언제 끝나니? → _____ does the test finish?

1. _____ (did, play, basketball, where, they)

2. _____ (do, like, why, this scarf, you)

3. _____ (the bakery, is, where)

4. _____ (did, when, hurt, John, his finger)

5. _____ (were, last Friday, you, where)

6. _____ (does, close, the bookstore, when)

7. _____ (like, the actress, you, why, do)

 Words trip 여행   vacation 휴가, 방학   Spanish 스페인어   excited 신난   bakery 빵집   finger 손가락

15 | how, how + 형용사/부사

1. how

· how는 '어떻게'라는 뜻으로 상태, 방법 등을 물을 때 쓴다.

How is the weather? 오늘 날씨는 어때?

– It's very cloudy. 매우 흐려.

How do you go to school? 너는 학교에 어떻게 가니?

– I go to school by bike. 나는 자전거를 타고 가.

Check 1 다음 우리말과 같은 뜻이 되도록 빈칸에 알맞은 말을 쓰시오.

1. 뉴욕의 날씨는 어떠니?

→ _____ _____ the weather in New York?

2. 그는 그 미술관에 어떻게 가니?

→ _____ _____ _____ go to the gallery?

---

2. how + 형용사/부사

· How + 형용사/부사 ~?는 '얼마나 ~하니?'라는 뜻으로 수나 양, 정도를 물을 때 쓴다.

How many ~?	〈수〉 ~ 얼마나 많니?	**How many** monkeys are there? – There are five monkeys.
How much ~?	〈양, 가격〉 ~ 얼마니?	**How much** milk do you want? – I want a glass of milk.
How old ~?	〈나이〉 ~ 몇 살이니?	**How old** is your daughter? – She is ten years old.
How often ~?	〈빈도〉 얼마나 자주 ~하니?	**How often** do you eat out? – Every day.
How long ~?	〈길이, 기간〉 ~ 얼마나 기니? 얼마나 오래 ~하니?	**How long** is this rope? – It is four meters long.
How tall ~?	〈키, 높이〉 ~ 얼마나 크니?	**How tall** are you? – I'm 170 centimeters.
How far ~?	〈거리, 정도〉 ~ 얼마나 멀리 있니?	**How far** is the theater from here? – It is about 1 kilometer.

Check 2 다음 괄호 안에서 알맞은 것을 고르시오.

1. (How many / How much) is this jacket?　　– It's 20 dollars.

2. (How long / How far) is the snake?　　– It's two meters long.

3. (How tall / How often) do you go there?　　– Once a month.

Practice 1   다음 〈보기〉에서 알맞은 말을 골라 빈칸에 쓰시오.

〈보기〉   long   tall   far   often   many   much   old

1. How _____ is this bridge? (이 다리는 얼마나 기니?)

2. How _____ cheese do you need? (너는 치즈가 얼마나 필요하니?)

3. How _____ is the station from here? (그 역은 여기서 얼마나 머니?)

4. How _____ is your younger sister? (네 여동생은 몇 살이니?)

5. How _____ is that old tower? (저 오래된 탑은 얼마나 높니?)

6. How _____ cities does she visit? (그녀는 얼마나 많은 도시를 방문하니?)

7. How _____ do you brush your teeth? (너는 얼마나 자주 양치질을 하니?)

Practice 2   다음 괄호 안에서 알맞은 것을 골라 빈칸에 쓰시오.

1. How _____ is this backpack? (much, many)

2. How _____ is the post office from here? (long, far)

3. How _____ puppies do you have? (much, many)

4. _____ tall is your father? (How, Who)

5. _____ was the weather yesterday? (How, What)

6. How _____ do you go to the library? (often, many)

7. How _____ does it take to the hospital? (long, far)

Practice 3   다음 대화의 빈칸에 알맞은 말을 쓰시오.

1. _____ was your vacation?   – It was great.

2. _____ does it take?   – It's about one hour.

3. _____ sheep are there on the farm? – Thirteen sheep.

4. _____ is that tree?   – It's 70 years old.

5. _____ do you go to the movies?   – Once a week.

6. _____ does she play tennis?   – For two hours.

7. _____ is the pretty woman?   – She is 171 centimeters.

 Words   bridge 다리   tower 탑   backpack 배낭   post office 우체국   farm 농장   tennis 테니스

A. 다음 빈칸에 알맞은 말을 〈보기〉에서 골라 쓰시오.

〈보기〉 Who   Whose   When   Which   How

1. _____ sweater is that?

2. _____ many onions do you want?

3. _____ do you like better, skiing or swimming?

4. _____ does your class begin?

B. 다음 우리말과 같도록 빈칸에 알맞은 말을 쓰시오.

1. 네가 가장 좋아하는 배우는 누구니?
   → _____ _____ your favorite actor?

2. 그녀는 왜 그렇게 일찍 떠났니?
   → _____ _____ she leave so early?

3. 그는 그의 가방을 어디서 잃어버렸니?
   → _____ _____ he lose his bag?

C. 다음 대답의 밑줄 친 부분을 참고하여 알맞은 질문을 쓰시오.

1. A: _____ (how often)
   B: I clean my room once a week.

2. A: _____ (how tall)
   B: She is 165 centimeters.

3. A: _____ (when)
   B: I get up at 6 o'clock every day.

D. 다음 대화의 빈칸에 알맞은 말을 쓰시오.

1. A: _____ _____ you eat dinner yesterday?
   B: I ate dinner at the restaurant.

2. A: _____ _____ the letter to him?
   B: Julia wrote the letter to him.

3. A: _____ _____ goes to the city hall?
   B: Bus No. 31.

4. A: _____ _____ you late for the party?
   B: Because I missed the train.

1. 다음 대화의 빈칸에 알맞은 것은?

> A: _____ was the festival?
> B: It was fantastic.

① Where   ② How
③ When   ④ Why
⑤ Which

2. 다음 중 밑줄 친 부분의 쓰임이 잘못된 것은?

① When is his birthday?
② Where does she live?
③ Whose gloves are they?
④ Why are you so sad?
⑤ Who are your hobbies?

3. 다음 우리말을 바르게 영작한 것은?

> 당신은 접시가 몇 개 필요합니까?

① How much plates do you need?
② How many plates do you need?
③ What plates do you need?
④ Which plates do you need?
⑤ Why do you need plates?

4. 다음 중 빈칸에 What이 들어갈 수 없는 것은?

① _____ is your address?
② _____ does she want?
③ _____ is your favorite fruit?
④ _____ did you do last night?
⑤ _____ do you go to the museum?

5. 다음 대화의 빈칸에 알맞지 않는 것은?

> A: Whose jacket is this?
> B: It's _____.

① mine   ② my brother's
③ his   ④ hers
⑤ Jake

6. 다음 빈칸에 공통으로 알맞은 의문사를 쓰시오.

> · _____ drew that picture?
> · _____ did you meet at the store?

→ _____

7. 다음 질문에 대한 대답으로 알맞은 것은?

> How long is the movie?

① It's about two hours.
② It's 30 centimeters long.
③ It's 50 years old.
④ It's three kilometers.
⑤ It's five thousand won.

8. 다음 대화의 빈칸에 들어갈 말이 바르게 짝지어진 것은?

> A: _____ were you late for school?
> B: Because I got up late.
> A: _____ did you get up?
> B: At 8:30.

① What – How   ② Why – Where
③ How – What   ④ Why – When
⑤ Which – When

[9-10] 다음 중 어법상 어색한 것을 고르시오.

9. ① How old is that tree?
   ② How often do you eat out?
   ③ How much is this hat?
   ④ How far is the store from here?
   ⑤ How long is your sister?

10. ① How is it going?
    ② Where are you, Jane?
    ③ What grade are you in?
    ④ Who is your favorite subject?
    ⑤ Why do many people like Toby?

[11-12] 다음 문장의 빈칸에 알맞은 것을 고르시오.

11. _____ is your bag?

   ① Where   ② How often
   ③ Why   ④ Who
   ⑤ When

12. Why _____ she angry at him?

   ① do   ② does
   ③ did   ④ is
   ⑤ are

13. 다음 질문에 대한 자연스러운 대답은?

   When do you sleep at night?

   ① At 11 o'clock.   ② By subway.
   ③ I get up early.   ④ Yes, I do.
   ⑤ I am a baker.

14. 다음 중 빈칸에 들어갈 말이 다른 것은?
   ① How _____ rulers do you have?
   ② How _____ money do you need?
   ③ How _____ brothers does he have?
   ④ How _____ horses are there?
   ⑤ How _____ pencils do you want?

15. 다음 문장의 빈칸에 알맞은 것은?

   How _____ do you exercise a day?
   너는 하루에 얼마나 오래 운동하니?

   ① far   ② tall
   ③ long   ④ old
   ⑤ often

16. 다음 중 밑줄 친 부분이 잘못된 것은?
   ① How long do you study math?
   ② How often do you visit him?
   ③ How many bread do you need?
   ④ How long is the bridge?
   ⑤ How many pigs do they have?

조동사란 무엇인가?
be동사나 일반동사 앞에서 동사의 의미가 더해지도록 도와주는 동사를 조동사라고 한다. 동사만으로 '~할 수 있다', '~할 것이다'와 같은 의미를 나타낼 수 없기 때문에 가능이나, 미래, 추측 등을 나타낼 때 조동사의 도움을 받아야 한다.

조동사의 특징은 무엇인가?
조동사는 도와주는 동사이기 때문에 반드시 be동사나 일반동사와 같이 쓰고, 조동사 뒤에는 항상 동사원형이 온다.

Chapter 6. 조동사

Unit

16 | can, will, may

1. can

· can은 '~할 수 있다'라는 뜻으로 능력이나 가능을 나타낸다.

I **can** speak Chinese. 나는 중국어를 말할 수 있다.

He **cannot[can't]** go with me. 그는 나와 함께 갈 수 없다.

Can you solve this problem? 너는 이 문제를 풀 수 있니?

– Yes, I can. / No, I can't.

＊능력이나 가능을 나타내는 can은 be able to로 바꿔 쓸 수 있다.

I **am able to** speak Chinese.

· '~해도 좋다, ~해 주시겠어요?'라는 뜻으로 허락이나 요청을 나타낸다.

You **can** use my cell phone. 너는 나의 휴대전화를 사용해도 좋다.

Can I go now? 제가 지금 가도 될까요?

– Yes, you can. 〈허가〉 / No, you can't. 〈불허〉

2. will

· will은 '~할 것이다, ~일 것이다'라는 뜻으로 미래에 대한 예정이나 의지를 나타낸다.

I **will** go to the concert tomorrow. 나는 내일 콘서트에 갈 것이다.

He **will not[won't]** come to the party. 그는 파티에 오지 않을 것이다.

＊will이 미래를 나타낼 때는 be going to로 바꿔 쓸 수 있다.

＊will과 can을 같이 써야 하는 경우에는 can을 be able to로 바꾸어 나타낸다.

I **will be able to** go to the concert.

· '~해 주시겠어요?'라는 뜻으로 상대방에 대한 요청이나 제안을 나타낸다.

Will you open the door? 문을 열어주시겠어요?

– Yes, I, will.[Sure. / Certainly.] 〈승낙〉 / Sorry, I can't. 〈거절〉

Check 1 다음 괄호 안에서 알맞은 것을 고르시오.

1. Can you (read / reading) this difficult book?

2. He (will / wills) meet them next weekend.

3. She (cannot / not can) play the guitar well.

---

3. may

· may는 '~일지도 모른다'라는 뜻으로 추측을 나타낸다.

He **may** be sick. 그는 아플지도 모른다.

· '~해도 좋다'라는 뜻으로 허락을 나타낸다.

May I come in? 제가 들어가도 될까요?

– Yes, you may. 〈허가〉 / No, you may not. 〈불허〉

Check 2 다음 우리말과 같은 뜻이 되도록 알맞은 것을 고르시오.

1. She (may / can) be Tom's mother. 그녀는 Tom의 어머니일지도 모른다.

2. (Will / May) I borrow your book? 내가 너의 책을 빌려도 될까?

Practice 1 다음 괄호 안에서 알맞은 것을 고르시오.

1. My sister can (drive, drives) a car.

2. She will (clean, cleans) her room.

3. His brother may (is, be) sick.

4. Her father will (read, reads) a newspaper.

5. We can (drink, drinking) some water.

6. My brother (goes, go) to the post office.

7. He (swim, swims) in this lake.

Practice 2 다음 괄호 안의 단어를 바르게 배열하여 문장을 완성하시오.

1. _____ pizza for dinner now. (she, make, can)

2. _____ me now? (help, can, you)

3. _____ difficult. (may, be, not, the test)

4. _____ this afternoon. (to, go, Japan, he, may)

5. _____ there today. (may, they, get)

6. _____ your dictionary? (use, I, may)

7. _____ on the light? (the baby, turn, can)

Practice 3 다음 괄호 안의 조동사를 넣어 문장을 다시 쓰시오.

1. I plant trees in the garden. (will) → _____

2. They go to Paris by airplane. (will) → _____

3. She is late for the meeting. (may) → _____

4. Bill studies hard for the exam. (will) → _____

5. My friend and I go shopping. (can) → _____

6. I wait for Ann at the bus stop. (can) → _____

7. He reads books in the library. (may) → _____

 Words drive 운전하다 lake 호수 difficult 어려운 light 전등 plant 심다 exam 시험 bus stop 버스 정류장

17 must, have to, should

1. must

· must는 '~해야 한다, ~할 필요가 있다'라는 뜻으로 의무나 필요를 나타낸다.

I **must** finish my homework. 나는 숙제를 끝내야만 한다.

You **must** not park here. 너는 여기에 주차해서는 안 된다.

· '~임에 틀림없다'라는 뜻으로 강한 추측을 나타낸다.

He **must** be tired. 그는 피곤한 게 틀림없다.

Anna **must** be at home. Anna는 집에 있는 게 틀림없다.

2. have to

· have to는 '~해야 한다, ~할 필요가 있다'라는 뜻으로 의무나 필요를 나타낸다. 주어가 3인칭 단수일 경우에는 has to로 쓰며, 과거는 had to로 쓴다.

I **have to** get up early tomorrow. 나는 내일 일찍 일어나야 한다.

She **has to** clean her room. 그녀는 방을 청소해야 한다.

I **don't have to** wear a coat. 나는 코트를 입을 필요가 없다.

I **must not** wear a coat. 나는 코트를 입어서는 안된다.

＊don't have to는 '~할 필요가 없다'라는 뜻의 불필요를 나타낸다.

＊must not은 '~해서는 안 된다'라는 뜻의 금지를 나타낸다.

· 부정문과 의문문 : 일반동사와 같은 방법으로 do[does/did]를 이용하여 만든다.

Do I **have to** call Jane? 내가 Jane에게 전화해야 하니?

– Yes, you **have to**. / No, you don't have to.

Does he **have to** go now? 그는 지금 가야 하니?

Check 1 다음 문장에서 <u>어색한</u> 부분을 찾아 고치시오.

1. He must not plays computer games.

2. She have to meet them in the park.

3. Do Tom have to wash the car today?

---

3. should

· should는 '~해야 한다, ~하는 게 좋겠다'라는 뜻으로 충고나 의무를 나타낸다.

I **should** take care of my sister. 나는 여동생을 돌봐야 한다.

We **should not[shouldn't]** eat too much. 우리는 과식해서는 안 된다.

You **should** take a rest at home. 너는 집에서 쉬는 게 좋겠다.

Check 2 다음 괄호 안에서 알맞은 것을 고르시오.

1. You look tired. You should go to bed (early / late).

2. My mother is sick. I (should / shouldn't) take care of her.

다음 괄호 안에서 알맞은 것을 골라 빈칸에 쓰시오.

1. You must _____ your homework. (do, did)

2. Mary doesn't have to _____ the book. (buy, buys)

3. We have to _____ old people. (help, helping)

4. You must not _____ pictures here. (take, took)

5. He has to _____ up early tomorrow. (get, gets)

6. We don't have to _____ up. (hurry, hurried)

7. People must not _____ lies. (tell, tells)

다음 우리말과 같도록 괄호 안의 단어들을 바르게 배열하시오.

1. 나는 나의 개를 산책시켜야만 한다.
   → _____ my dog. (to, have, I, walk)

2. 우리는 약속을 지켜야만 한다.
   → _____ the promise. (must, we, keep)

3. 그들은 늦게까지 공부해야만 한다.
   → They _____. (late, must, study)

4. 그 아기는 배고픈 것이 틀림없다.
   → The baby _____. (be, hungry, must)

5. 그 여자는 최선을 다해야 한다.
   → _____ her best. (the woman, do, to, has)

6. 우리는 정직해야만 한다.
   → We _____. (honest, must, be)

7. 그는 변호사임에 틀림없다.
   → He _____. (be, lawyer, must, a)

다음 문장의 밑줄 친 부분을 바르게 고치시오.

1. She not should turn right.   → _____

2. He should exercises every day.   → _____

3. Mike have to go home early.   → _____

4. We should not ate junk food.   → _____

5. He has to takes care of his brother. → _____

6. They should are quiet in public.   → _____

7. You shouldn't crosses the street here. → _____

Words hurry 서두르다   lie 거짓말하다   promise 약속   lawyer 변호사   junk food 불량 식품   cross 건너다

A. 다음 우리말과 같도록 알맞은 조동사를 쓰시오.

1. 타조들은 새이다. 그러나 그들은 날 수 없다.
   → Ostriches are birds. But they _____ fly.

2. 지금 날씨가 흐리다. 곧 비가 올지도 모른다.
   → It's cloudy now. It _____ rain soon.

3. 그 남자는 그 모자를 쓸 필요가 없다.
   → The man _____ wear the cap.

4. 그녀는 열이 있다. 그녀는 아픈 것이 틀림없다.
   → She has a fever. She _____ be sick.

B. 다음 문장을 괄호 안의 지시대로 바꾸시오.

1. Nick has to wait for the truck. (의문문으로)
   → _____

2. You should leave here now. (부정문으로)
   → _____

3. It will be sunny this afternoon. (의문문으로)
   → _____

4. She has to work next Sunday. (She를 I로)
   → _____

C. 다음 문장의 밑줄 친 부분을 바르게 고치시오.

1. They <u>not must</u> swim in the deep sea.

2. You <u>has to</u> be quiet in the classroom.

3. He <u>don't</u> have to tell her about it.

4. She won't <u>listens</u> to the radio at night.

D. 다음 빈칸에 들어갈 말로 알맞은 것을 고르시오.

> Jamie is a middle school student. He won't go to school next Monday because it is Children's Day. He _____ get up early next Monday.

① have to   ② doesn't have to

③ must not   ④ should not

Words

A. cloudy 흐린
soon 곧
fever 열
sick 아픈

B. truck 트럭
leave 떠나다
sunny 화창한

C. deep 깊은
quiet 조용한
radio 라디오

D. Children's Day 어린이날
because ~ 때문에

[1-2] 다음 중 빈칸에 들어갈 알맞은 것을 고르시오.

1.
> I _____ play the guitar very well.

① can   ② does
③ is   ④ not
⑤ doesn't

2.
> He _____ be ten years old next year.

① do   ② is
③ will   ④ don't
⑤ doesn't

[3-4] 다음 문장의 빈칸에 공통으로 알맞은 것을 고르시오.

3.
> · She _____ be tired.
> · _____ I use your pencil?

① does   ② do
③ have   ④ may
⑤ won't

4.
> · The boy _____ be sick.
> · I'm late. I _____ hurry.

① can   ② don't
③ won't   ④ have
⑤ must

5. 다음 문장의 밑줄 친 부분과 바꿔 쓸 수 있는 것은?

> Sally must tell the truth.

① have to   ② may
③ can   ④ will
⑤ has to

6. 다음 빈칸에 알맞은 것은?

> You _____ brush your teeth before you go to bed.

① have   ② has
③ have to   ④ has to
⑤ don't have

7. 다음 의문문에 대한 대답으로 알맞은 것은?

> Can you ride a bike well?

① Yes, I do.   ② Yes, I will.
③ No, I don't.   ④ No, I can.
⑤ No, I can't.

8. 다음 문장에 will을 넣어 잘 나타낸 것은?

> I can travel around the world.

① I will travel around the world.
② I will can travel around the world.
③ I will able to travel around the world.
④ I will be able to travel around the world.
⑤ I will am able to travel around the world.

9. 다음 빈칸에 알맞지 <u>않는</u> 것은?

> Ron can _____.

① go to the party　② buy a book
③ play with her　④ rides a bike
⑤ help them

10. 다음 빈칸에 공통으로 알맞은 말을 쓰시오.

> · The boy _____ be sad.
> (그 소년은 슬플지도 모른다.)
> · _____ I turn off the light?
> (제가 불을 꺼도 될까요?)

→ _____

11. 다음 중 어법상 알맞은 것은?
① Jack will is fine.
② She must go to the library.
③ You should listens to him.
④ He may be not hungry.
⑤ Can you gave me a hand?

12. 다음 대화의 밑줄 친 부분의 의도로 알맞은 것은?

> A: I caught a bad cold.
> B: Oh, that's too bad.
> <u>You should go to see a doctor.</u>

① 허락　② 추측
③ 충고　④ 가능
⑤ 능력

13. 다음 〈보기〉의 밑줄 친 부분과 의미가 <u>다른</u> 것은?

> 〈보기〉 You <u>may</u> need our help.

① He may be in his room.
② Her sister may be upset.
③ You may play outside.
④ It may snow this afternoon.
⑤ She may watch a movie.

14. 다음 밑줄 친 부분의 쓰임이 나머지와 <u>다른</u> 것은?
① She <u>must</u> go home right now.
② You <u>must</u> come back by 8.
③ They <u>must</u> leave early.
④ We <u>must</u> be kind to the people.
⑤ He <u>must</u> be very sleepy.

15. 다음 밑줄 친 부분 중 어법상 <u>어색한</u> 것은?
① <u>Can you send</u> me a letter?
② She <u>wills be</u> fine.
③ Steve <u>should not</u> eat fast food.
④ He <u>must be</u> very thirsty.
⑤ You <u>may use</u> my computer.

16. 다음 대화의 빈칸에 알맞은 것은?

> A: Can you play the guitar?
> B: _____ But I can play the piano.

① Yes, I can.　② No, I can't.
③ Yes, you can.　④ No, we can.
⑤ Yes, we can't.

형용사란 무엇인가?

형용사는 명사 앞에서 명사를 꾸며 주거나 be동사와 함께 쓰여 주어를 보충 설명해 주는 역할을 한다. 형용사에는 지시형용사, 수량형용사, 성질을 나타내는 형용사가 있다.

부사란 무엇인가?

부사는 동사, 형용사, 다른 부사 등을 꾸며 주는 말로, 형용사 앞이나 문장 뒤에 오며 문장을 강조할 때는 문장 앞에 오기도 한다. 빈도를 나타내는 부사를 빈도부사라고 하는데 빈도부사는 be동사나 조동사 뒤에, 일반동사 앞에 위치한다.

Chapter 7. 형용사와 부사

18 │ 형용사

1. 형용사의 역할

· 형용사는 명사 앞에서 명사를 수식한다.

Jenny is a **pretty** girl. Jenny는 예쁜 소녀이다.

It is a **big** dog. 그것은 큰 개다.

· 형용사는 be동사 뒤에서 주어의 상태나 성질을 설명한다.

Jenny is **pretty**. Jenny는 예쁘다.

The dog is **big**. 그 개는 크다.

Check 1 다음 두 문장의 의미가 같도록 빈칸에 알맞은 말을 쓰시오.

1. This is a big house. = This house is _____.

2. She is a famous actress. = The actress is _____.

3. Kevin is a very kind boy. = Kevin is very _____.

---

2. 수와 양을 나타내는 형용사

· many, much는 '많은'이라는 뜻으로 many는 셀 수 있는 명사의 복수형 앞에, much는 셀 수 없는 명사 앞에 쓰인다.

I have **many** friends. 나는 많은 친구들이 있다.

I don't have **much** money. 나는 돈이 많이 없다.

· many와 much는 a lot of, lots of로 바꿔 쓸 수 있다. a lot of, lots of는 셀 수 있는 명사와 셀 수 없는 명사 앞에 모두 쓸 수 있다.

I have **a lot of** flowers. 나는 많은 꽃들을 가지고 있다.

I have **a lot of** money. 나는 많은 돈을 가지고 있다.

＊much의 경우 보통 부정문과 의문문에 쓰이고 긍정문에는 a lot of를 쓴다. much를 긍정문에 쓸 경우에는 so, too, very와 같은 말과 함께 쓴다.

· some, any는 '약간의, 몇몇의'라는 뜻으로 셀 수 있는 명사와 셀 수 없는 명사 앞에 모두 쓸 수 있다. some은 긍정문에 쓰이고 any는 부정문과 의문문에 쓰인다. 단, 권유문의 경우 의문문의 형태이지만 some을 쓴다.

There is **some** water in the bottle. 그 병에 약간의 물이 있다. (긍정문)

Would you want **some** milk? 우유 좀 마실래요? (권유문)

I don't have **any** sisters. 나는 여자 형제들이 없다. (부정문)

Do you have **any** sugar? 약간의 설탕이 있나요? (의문문)

Check 2 다음 괄호 안에서 알맞은 것을 고르시오.

1. She has (many / much) dogs.

2. They don't have (many / much) time.

3. I want (some / any) apples and oranges.

다음 두 문장의 의미가 같도록 빈칸에 알맞은 말을 쓰시오.

1. The man is handsome.　　= He is a _____.

2. The movie is exciting.　　= It is an _____.

3. The singers are popular.　= _____

4. The woman is beautiful.　= _____

5. The peach is fresh.　　　= _____

6. The car is expensive.　　= _____

7. The gloves are cheap.　　= _____

다음 괄호 안에서 알맞은 것을 고르시오.

1. There isn't (some / any) juice in the bottle.

2. (Many / Much) people went to the festival.

3. I don't have (some / any) notebooks.

4. Would you like (some / many) milk?

5. She has (many / much) backpacks.

6. We don't need (many / much) money.

7. Do you have (some / any) plans this holiday?

다음 우리말과 같도록 괄호 안의 단어들을 이용하여 문장을 완성하시오.

1. 저 작은 원숭이를 봐! (that, monkey, small)

   → _____

2. 나는 검정색 모자를 샀다. (a, cap, black, bought)

   → _____

3. 그는 멋진 정원을 가지고 있다. (nice, has, a, garden)

   → _____

4. 그 고양이는 작고 귀엽다. (cute, is, small, and)

   → _____

5. 그 소녀는 큰 눈을 가지고 있다. (has, eyes, big)

   → _____

6. 그 여자는 새 신발을 원한다. (new, wants, shoes)

   → _____

Words　handsome 잘생긴　popular 인기 있는　peach 복숭아　festival 축제　plan 계획　holiday 휴일, 휴가

19 부사

1. 부사의 역할

· 부사는 동사, 형용사, 다른 부사, 또는 문장 전체를 수식한다.

Eric walks **slowly**. Eric은 천천히 걷는다. (동사 수식)

It is **really** cold today. 오늘 정말 춥다. (형용사 수식)

Ashley likes her dog **very** much. Ashley는 그녀의 개를 매우 많이 좋아한다. (부사 수식)

Luckily, I passed the exam. 운 좋게 나는 그 시험에 합격했다. (문장 전체 수식)

2. 부사의 형태

· 부사는 보통 형용사에 -ly를 붙여서 만든다.

대부분의 경우	형용사+-ly	beautiful → beautifully, slow → slowly, nice → nicely, wise → wisely
자음+y로 끝나는 경우	y를 i로 고치고+-ly	happy → happily, easy → easily, lucky → luckily, heavy → heavily
-le, -ue로 끝나는 경우	e를 빼고+-y	simple → simply, true → truly
형용사와 부사의 형태가 같은 경우	fast, late, early, near, far, high, low, much, enough, long, hard, …	
형용사와 부사의 형태가 다른 경우	good → well	

> **Check 1** 다음 형용사의 부사형을 쓰시오.
>
> 1. bad   → _____
> 2. easy   → _____
> 3. late   → _____
> 4. good   → _____
> 5. long   → _____
> 6. simple   → _____

3. 빈도부사

· 빈도부사는 빈도나 횟수를 나타내는 부사로 일반동사 앞에, be동사나 조동사 뒤에 위치한다.

always	>	usually	>	often	>	sometimes	>	never
(항상, 늘)		(보통, 대개)		(자주, 종종)		(때때로, 가끔)		(결코 ~ 않다)

He **always** walks his dog after dinner. 그는 저녁 식사 후에 항상 개를 산책시킨다.

It is **usually** warm in spring. 봄에는 보통 따뜻하다.

Do you **often** go to the bookstore? 너는 서점에 자주 가니?

They will **never** eat fast food. 그들은 패스트푸드를 결코 먹지 않을 것이다.

> **Check 2** 다음 우리말과 같도록 빈칸에 알맞은 말을 쓰시오.
>
> 1. She is _____ late for school. 그녀는 가끔 지각을 한다.
> 2. I _____ play baseball. 나는 종종 야구를 한다.
> 3. He _____ tells a lie. 그는 결코 거짓말을 하지 않는다.

1. The people smile _____. (happy, happily)

2. The child eats soup _____. (slow, slowly)

3. Fatty food is _____. (dangerous, dangerously)

4. They are very _____ (good, well) athletes.

5. The child goes to school _____. (late, lately)

6. The cat jumps down _____. (quick, quickly)

7. The woman speaks English _____. (good, well)

Practice 2 | 다음 빈도부사의 알맞은 위치를 고르시오.

1. My son ① goes ② to ③ school ④ early. (always)

2. I ① wash ② my hair ③ once ④ a day. (usually)

3. She ① will ② sing ③ a song ④ on the stage. (never)

4. My mom ① makes ② chocolate ③ cake ④. (sometimes)

5. He ① is ② late ③ for ④ school. (never)

6. He ① can ② use ③ the ④ chopsticks. (usually)

7. My family ① goes ② to ③ the theater ④. (often)

Practice 3 | 다음 밑줄 친 부분을 바르게 고치시오.

1. She opened the door slow.   → _____

2. The owl is flying highly in the sky.   → _____

3. It is hot really today.   → _____

4. I found the store easy.   → _____

5. My father goes often fishing at night. → _____

6. He didn't sleep good last night.   → _____

7. It rained heavy yesterday.   → _____

 soup 수프   fatty 기름진   dangerous 위험한   athlete 운동선수   chopsticks 젓가락   owl 올빼미

20 비교급과 최상급

1. 비교급과 최상급의 역할

· 비교 대상이 둘인 경우에는 비교급을 사용하고, 셋 이상인 경우에는 최상급을 사용한다.

	비교급	최상급	예
대부분의 형용사나 부사	원급+-er	원급+-est	fast – faster – fastest, long – longer – longest
-e로 끝나는 경우	원급+-r	원급+-st	large – larger – largest, nice – nicer – nicest
자음+-y로 끝나는 경우	y를 i로 고치고 +-er	y를 i로 고치고 +-est	easy – easier – easiest, happy – happier – happiest
단모음+단자음으로 끝나는 1음절의 경우	마지막 자음을 한 번 더 쓰고 +-er	마지막 자음을 한 번 더 쓰고 +-est	big – bigger – biggest, hot – hotter – hottest
-ed, -ing, -ful, -less, -ous로 끝나거나 3음절 이상인 경우	more+원급	most+원급	famous – more famous – most famous, useful – more useful – most useful
불규칙 변화	good/well – better – best, bad/badly – worse – worst, many/much – more – most, little – less – least		

Check 1 다음 단어의 비교급과 최상급을 쓰시오.

1. pretty – _____ – _____

2. exciting – _____ – _____

2. 원급 비교

· 「as+형용사[부사]의 원급+as」의 형태로 '～만큼 …한[하게]'이라는 뜻을 가지며, 비교하는 대상의 정도가 같음을 나타낸다.

Tina is **as** tall **as** Mary. Tina는 Mary만큼 키가 크다.

· 부정문은 「not as[so]+형용사[부사]의 원급+as」의 형태로 '～만큼 …하지 않은'이라는 뜻이다.

I am **not as[so]** fast **as** Jimmy. 나는 Jimmy만큼 빠르지 않다.

3. 비교급과 최상급 문장

· 비교급은 「비교급+than」의 형태로 '～보다 …한[하게]'이라는 뜻으로 둘을 비교한다.

A watermelon is **bigger than** an apple. 수박은 사과보다 크다.

· 최상급은 「the+최상급」의 형태로 '가장 …한[하게]'이라는 뜻으로 셋 이상의 대상을 비교한다.

Lucy is **the smartest** girl in the class. Lucy는 반에서 가장 똑똑한 소녀이다.

He is **the most famous** singer of the three. 그는 그 셋 중에서 가장 유명한 가수이다.

*최상급 문장에서 in 뒤에는 범위나 소속이 오고 of 뒤에는 대상이 온다.

Check 2 다음 괄호 안에서 알맞은 것을 고르시오.

1. I am (older / oldest) than Luke.

2. Ryan is the (heavier / heaviest) boy of all the students.

3. Andrew is as (popular / more popular) as his brother.

Practice 1 | 다음 단어의 비교급과 최상급을 쓰시오.

1. rich – ＿＿＿＿＿＿ – ＿＿＿＿＿＿

2. big – ＿＿＿＿＿＿ – ＿＿＿＿＿＿

3. good – ＿＿＿＿＿＿ – ＿＿＿＿＿＿

4. large – ＿＿＿＿＿＿ – ＿＿＿＿＿＿

5. much – ＿＿＿＿＿＿ – ＿＿＿＿＿＿

6. useful – ＿＿＿＿＿＿ – ＿＿＿＿＿＿

7. bad – ＿＿＿＿＿＿ – ＿＿＿＿＿＿

Practice 2 | 다음 괄호 안의 단어를 알맞은 형태로 바꿔 쓰시오.

1. This building is the ＿＿＿＿＿＿ in this city. (big)

2. The star looks ＿＿＿＿＿＿ than the others. (bright)

3. This bag is ＿＿＿＿＿＿ than that one. (heavy)

4. The North Pole is ＿＿＿＿＿＿ than Korea. (cold)

5. Your puppy is the ＿＿＿＿＿＿ of the four. (cute)

6. You are the ＿＿＿＿＿＿ mother in the world. (good)

7. He is the ＿＿＿＿＿＿ man in our town. (brave)

Practice 3 | 다음 밑줄 친 부분을 바르게 고쳐 쓰시오.

1. It is the longer bridge in the world. → ＿＿＿＿＿＿

2. Sam is the most smart student in his class. → ＿＿＿＿＿＿

3. I'm as younger as Jane. → ＿＿＿＿＿＿

4. The necklace is the more expensive of all. → ＿＿＿＿＿＿

5. He is as strongest as his father. → ＿＿＿＿＿＿

6. She is the more famous singer in Canada. → ＿＿＿＿＿＿

7. January is coldest than December. → ＿＿＿＿＿＿

Words useful 유용한 bright 밝은 North Pole 북극 brave 용감한 bridge 다리 necklace 목걸이

A. 다음 문장의 괄호 안에서 알맞은 것을 고르시오.

1. Do you have (some / any) pencils?

2. There are (much / a lot of) oranges in the basket.

3. Don't spend (many / much) time on computer games.

4. Would you like (some / any) juice?

Words

A. basket 바구니
   spend 쓰다, 소비하다

B. 다음 괄호 안의 단어를 넣어 문장을 다시 쓰시오.

1. Nick exercises in the gym. (often)

   → _____

2. She can find her hairpin. (never)

   → _____

3. It is rainy and hot in summer. (usually)

   → _____

4. My sister goes to the library on Sunday. (always)

   → _____

B. exercise 운동하다
   gym 체육관
   hairpin 머리핀

C. 다음 밑줄 친 부분을 바르게 고치시오.

1. I went to bed lately last night.   → _____

2. We can solve the problem easy.   → _____

3. The man speaks quiet.   → _____

4. She is a well tennis player.   → _____

C. solve 풀다
   quiet 조용한
   player 운동선수

D. 다음 우리말과 같도록 괄호 안의 단어를 이용하여 문장을 완성하시오.

1. 이 의자는 저 소파만큼 편하다. (comfortable)

   → This chair is as _____ that sofa.

2. 오늘은 어제만큼 춥지 않다. (cold)

   → Today is _____ as yesterday.

3. 제주도는 한국에서 가장 큰 섬이다. (large)

   → Jeju-do is _____ in Korea.

4. 그는 그의 남동생보다 더 인기가 있다. (popular)

   → He is _____ his brother.

D. comfortable 편안한
   sofa 소파
   island 섬

1. 다음 두 단어의 관계가 나머지와 <u>다른</u> 하나는?
   ① true – truly
   ② high – high
   ③ much – more
   ④ good – well
   ⑤ careful – carefully

2. 다음 중 비교급과 최상급이 <u>잘못</u> 연결된 것은?
   ① hot – hotter – hottest
   ② busy – busyer – busyest
   ③ long – longer – longest
   ④ well – better – best
   ⑤ happy – happier – happiest

3. 다음 단어의 성격이 나머지와 <u>다른</u> 것은?
   ① high
   ② safe
   ③ school
   ④ easy
   ⑤ happy

4. 다음 밑줄 친 fast의 쓰임이 나머지와 <u>다른</u> 것은?
   ① Joy is walking <u>fast</u> to the store.
   ② A cheetah is a <u>fast</u> animal.
   ③ My brother swam <u>fast</u> yesterday.
   ④ I have to finish my work <u>fast</u>.
   ⑤ That dog runs very <u>fast</u>.

5. 다음 밑줄 친 부분과 같은 것은?

   There are <u>a lot of</u> robots in my room.

   ① this
   ② any
   ③ some
   ④ much
   ⑤ many

6. 다음 빈칸에 들어갈 말이 바르게 짝지어진 것은?

   · Would you like _____ cookies?
   · There isn't _____ water in the glass.

   ① any – some
   ② any – any
   ③ some – many
   ④ some – any
   ⑤ much – some

7. 다음 중 밑줄 친 부분이 어법상 <u>어색한</u> 것은?
   ① Do not walk <u>slowly</u>.
   ② I have too <u>much</u> work.
   ③ This is a <u>heavy</u> box.
   ④ Sally doesn't have <u>many</u> sugar.
   ⑤ He studies math very <u>hard</u>.

8. 다음 중 밑줄 친 부사의 위치가 <u>잘못된</u> 것은?
   ① She is <u>usually</u> sad on rainy day.
   ② I <u>often</u> wash the dishes after dinner.
   ③ Does he <u>sometimes</u> call his parents?
   ④ My brother <u>always</u> swims with Anna.
   ⑤ Julia <u>never</u> will play the piano.

9. 다음 괄호 안의 단어를 넣어 문장을 다시 쓰시오.

> It is cold today. (really)

→ _____

10. 다음 빈칸에 들어갈 말이 나머지와 다른 것은?

① My feet are smaller _____ yours.
② She feels better _____ yesterday.
③ A cat is bigger _____ a mouse.
④ He is the best student _____ my class.
⑤ She runs faster _____ her sister.

11. 다음 빈칸에 알맞지 <u>않은</u> 것은?

> These are more _____ than those.

① useful   ② expensive
③ popular   ④ pretty
⑤ famous

12. 다음 문장의 빈칸에 들어갈 알맞은 말을 쓰시오.

> A doll is 8 dollars. A robot is 10 dollars.
> A robot is _____ than a doll.

→ _____

13. 다음 중 밑줄 친 부분이 <u>어색한</u> 것은?

① I made <u>much</u> kites.
② I have <u>many</u> friends.
③ There are <u>some</u> people.
④ Do you have <u>any</u> money?
⑤ We had <u>lots of</u> rain last year.

[14-15] 다음 중 자연스러운 문장은?

14. ① She drinks any coffee.
② Does she have some pens?
③ They eat much apples in the room.
④ They have some friends in Japan.
⑤ There is many water in the bottle.

15. ① She sometimes meets him.
② He always is happy.
③ They play often soccer.
④ He never will drink Coke.
⑤ I go usually to school at eight.

16. 다음 중 usually를 넣어 바르게 나타낸 것은?

> I have lunch at noon.

① I have lunch at usually noon.
② I usually have lunch at noon.
③ I have usually lunch at noon.
④ I have lunch usually at noon.
⑤ I have lunch at noon usually.

명령문과 청유문은 무엇인가?
상대방에게 어떤 행동을 하라고 명령하거나 지시하는 문장이 명령
문이다. 상대방에게 어떤 행동을 함께 하자고 제안하거나 권유하
는 문장이 청유문이다.

감탄문은 무엇인가?
감탄문은 놀라움이나 기쁨, 슬픔 등 감정을 표현하기 위한 문장이
다. What이나 How로 시작하고 문장의 끝에 느낌표(!)가 붙는다.

부가의문문과 선택의문문은 무엇인가?
부가의문문은 평서문이나 명령문 끝에 의문을 나타내는 표현을 붙
여서 상대방의 동의를 구하거나 사실을 확인하는 의문문이다. 선택
의문문은 선택을 묻는 의문문으로 대답은 Yes나 No로 하지 않고
둘 중 하나를 선택해서 답한다.

Chapter 8. 문장의 종류

21 | 명령문과 청유문

1. 명령문

• 명령문은 '~하시오, ~해라'라는 뜻으로 상대방에게 명령, 지시, 요청 등을 할 때 쓰며, 주어를 없애고 동사원형으로 문장을 시작한다.

You are quiet. → **Be** quiet. 조용히 해라.

You clean your room. → **Clean** your room. 너의 방을 청소해라.

＊명령문 뒤나 앞에 please를 붙이면 '~해 주세요'라는 뜻으로 공손한 표현이 된다. 또한 please를 뒤에 붙일 때는 please 앞에 ,(쉼표)를 붙여야 한다.

Clean your room, **please**. ＝**Please** clean your room. 너의 방을 청소하세요.

2. 부정명령문

• 부정명령문은 '~하지 마라'라는 뜻으로 주어를 없애고 「Don't+동사원형 ~.」으로 나타낸다.

You run in the classroom. 너는 교실에서 달린다. (평서문)

→ **Run** in the classroom. 교실에서 달려라. (명령문)

→ **Don't run** in the classroom. 교실에서 달리지 마라. (부정명령문)

Don't be afraid. 두려워하지 마라.

> ## Check 1 다음 괄호 안에서 알맞은 것을 고르시오.
> 1. (Wash / Washes) your hands.
> 2. (Don't be / Don't are) shy.
> 3. (Sit / Sits) down, please.

3. 청유문

• 청유문은 제안문이라고도 하며 '~하자'라는 뜻으로 상대방에게 제안을 할 때 쓰고, 「Let's+동사원형 ~.」으로 나타낸다.

Let's play soccer on the playground. 운동장에서 축구하자.

Let's go to the park in the afternoon. 오후에 공원에 가자.

• 청유문에 대한 대답은 긍정일 때는 Yes, let's. / Okay. / Why not? / That's a good idea. 등으로 하고, 부정일 때는 No, let's not. / I'm sorry, I can't. / I'm afraid I can't. 등으로 한다.

• '~하지 말자'라고 부정을 나타낼 때는 「Let's not+동사원형 ~.」으로 나타낸다.

Let's not eat out. 외식하지 말자.

Let's not stay here. 여기에 머무르지 말자.

> ## Check 2 다음 문장을 우리말로 옮기시오.
> 1. Let's take a walk.
> 2. Let's not eat the food.
> 3. Let's go fishing this weekend.

1. You open the window. → _____
2. You do your homework. → _____
3. You are kind to everyone. → _____
4. You put on your jacket. → _____
5. You drive the car slowly. → _____
6. You are quiet in the library. → _____
7. You make a birthday card. → _____

1. 오늘 여기를 떠나지 마라. (leave) = _____ here today.
2. 다시는 늦지 마라. (be) = _____ late again.
3. 그 모래성을 만들지 마라. (build) = _____ the sand castle.
4. 물을 낭비하지 마라. (waste) = _____ water.
5. 너무 크게 대화하지 마라. (talk) = _____ too loudly.
6. 강당에서 사진을 찍지 마라. (take) = _____ pictures in the hall.
7. 콜라를 너무 많이 마시지 마라. (drink) = _____ too much Coke.

1. Let's _____ on a picnic. (go, goes)
2. Let's _____ at the station. (meet, met)
3. Let's _____ baseball. (play, plays)
4. Let's not _____ out this weekend. (eat, eats)
5. Let's not _____ a noise here. (make, makes)
6. _____ play outside. It's very cold. (Let's, Let's not)
7. It's dangerous here. _____ cross the street. (Let's, Let's not)

 put on 입다   waste 낭비하다   Coke 콜라   picnic 소풍   dangerous 위험한   cross 건너다

22 감탄문

1. 감탄문

· 감탄문은 놀람이나 기쁨, 슬픔 등의 감정을 나타내는 문장이다. what이나 how로 시작하고 문장의 마지막에 !(느낌표)를 쓴다.

What a nice hat it is! 정말 멋진 모자구나!

How clever you are! 너는 정말 영리하구나!

2. What으로 시작하는 감탄문

· What으로 시작하는 감탄문은 명사를 강조할 때 사용하며 「What+a[an]+형용사+명사+(주어+동사)!」의 형태로 나타내고, 이때 「주어+동사」는 생략할 수 있다. 복수명사이거나 셀 수 없는 명사의 경우에는 a[an]를 쓰지 않는다.

It is a very big backpack. 그것은 매우 큰 배낭이다.

What a big backpack (it is)! 정말 큰 배낭이구나!
　　　a+형용사+명사　　(주어+동사)

What nice shoes they are! 정말 멋진 신발이구나! (shoes가 복수이므로 a[an] ×)

What delicious bread it is! 정말 맛있는 빵이구나! (bread가 셀 수 없는 명사이므로 a[an] ×)

> **Check 1** 다음 밑줄 친 부분을 바르게 고치시오.
>
> 1. What <u>pretty</u> girl she is!
> 2. What <u>a wonderful pants</u> they are!
> 3. What sweet cookies <u>it is</u>!

3. How로 시작하는 감탄문

· How로 시작하는 감탄문은 형용사를 강조할 때 사용하며 「How+형용사[부사]+(주어+동사)!」의 형태로 나타내고, 이때 「주어+동사」는 생략할 수 있다.

The clothes are very beautiful. 그 옷은 매우 아름답다.

How beautiful (the clothes are)! 정말 아름다운 옷이구나!
　　형용사　　　(주어+동사)

> **Check 2** 다음 빈칸에 How 또는 What을 쓰시오.
>
> 1. _____ tall the tree is!
> 2. _____ a scary movie it is!
> 3. _____ kind the man is!

다음 빈칸에 What 또는 How를 쓰시오.

1. _____ expensive it is!

2. _____ a big palace it is!

3. _____ brave the boy is!

4. _____ fresh oranges they are!

5. _____ an interesting book it is!

6. _____ beautiful the pictures are!

7. _____ a great concert it is!

Practice 2   다음 문장을 감탄문으로 바꿀 때 빈칸에 알맞은 말을 쓰시오.

1. It is a very old temple.   → _____ temple it is!

2. The frog jumps very high.   → _____ the frog jumps!

3. The luggage is very heavy.   → _____ the luggage is!

4. Harry comes very early.   → _____ Harry comes!

5. The rainbow is very beautiful.   → _____ the rainbow is!

6. She is a very busy woman.   → _____ woman she is!

7. They are very amazing stories.   → _____ stories they are!

Practice 3   다음 문장에서 틀린 부분에 밑줄을 긋고 바르게 고쳐 쓰시오.

1. How a funny book this is!   → _____

2. What interesting his class is!   → _____

3. What cute babies are they!   → _____

4. What a ugly dog that is!   → _____

5. How cold soup it is!   → _____

6. What small this stove is!   → _____

7. What a wise wife she is?   → _____

Words palace 궁전, 궁궐   temple 사찰, 절   luggage 짐   rainbow 무지개   amazing 놀라운   stove 난로

23 부가의문문과 선택의문문

1. 부가의문문

· '그렇지?, 그렇지 않니?'라는 뜻으로 상대방의 동의를 구하거나 사실을 확인하기 위해 평서문 끝에 「동사+주어(인칭대명사)?」의 형태로 짧게 붙인다.

　She is pretty, **isn't she**? 그녀는 예쁘지, 그렇지 않니?

· 만드는 법

　1) 앞 문장이 긍정문이면 부정으로, 부정문이면 긍정으로 부가의문문을 만든다.

　2) 앞 문장에 be동사와 조동사가 쓰였으면 그대로 쓰고, 일반동사가 쓰였으면 주어의 인칭과 수, 시제에 따라 do, does, did를 쓴다.

　　The movie is exciting, **isn't it**? 그 영화는 재미있지, 그렇지 않니?

　　He can't swim, **can he**? 그는 수영을 못하지, 그렇지?

　3) 앞 문장의 주어가 명사이면 인칭대명사로 바꿔 쓴다.

　　<u>David</u> <u>works</u> at a bank, <u>**doesn't**</u> <u>**he**</u>? David는 은행에서 일하지, 그렇지 않니?
　　　명사　긍정　　　　　　　부정　인칭대명사

· 부가의문문에 대한 대답 : 대답하는 내용이 긍정이면 Yes로, 부정이면 No로 답한다.

　You finished your homework, **didn't you**? 너는 너의 숙제를 끝냈지, 그렇지 않니?

　– Yes, I did. 응, 끝냈어. / No, I didn't. 아니, 안 끝냈어.

> **Check 1 다음 괄호 안에서 알맞은 것을 고르시오.**
> 1. You are sleepy, (are you / aren't you)?
> 2. Judy didn't visit Sam, (did Judy / did she)?
> 3. They will go on a trip, (will they / won't they)?

2. 선택의문문

· 선택의문문은 or를 써서 선택을 묻는 의문문으로 대답은 Yes나 No로 하지 않고 둘 중 하나를 선택해서 답한다.

　Do you go to school by bus **or** by bike? 너는 학교에 버스로 가니, 자전거로 가니?

　– I go to school by bike. 나는 자전거로 학교에 가.

　Which do you **want**, apples **or** bananas? 너는 사과와 바나나 중에 어느 것을 원하니?

　– I **want** apples. 나는 사과를 원해.

> **Check 2 다음 우리말과 같은 뜻이 되도록 빈칸에 알맞은 말을 쓰시오.**
> 1. 그 커피는 뜨겁니, 차갑니?
> 　→ Is the coffee hot _____ _____?
> 2. 넌 수학과 영어 중에서 어떤 걸 더 좋아하니?
> 　→ _____ do you like better, math _____ English?

Practice 1 　다음 괄호 안에서 알맞은 것을 고르시오.

1. This movie isn't for children, (is, isn't) it?

2. The actor was famous then, (was, wasn't) he?

3. You will climb the mountain, (will, won't) you?

4. These boxes weren't heavy, (were, are) they?

5. You didn't buy the big bag, (did, do) you?

6. He ate breakfast this morning, (did, didn't) he?

7. The dog can catch the ball, (can, can't) it?

Practice 2 　다음 빈칸에 알맞은 부가의문문을 쓰시오.

1. She won't have dinner today, _____?

2. You visited your uncle last month, _____?

3. Linda always helps her father, _____?

4. You and your brother are smart, _____?

5. Your daughter can play the violin well, _____?

6. You weren't at home yesterday, _____?

7. They didn't wash the car yesterday, _____?

Practice 3 　다음 우리말과 같은 뜻이 되도록 빈칸에 알맞은 말을 쓰시오.

1. 너의 남동생은 키가 크니, 키가 작니?
   → Is your brother tall _____ short?

2. 너는 수영을 즐기니, 조깅을 즐기니?
   → Do you enjoy swimming _____ jogging?

3. 너는 샐러드와 수프 중에서 어떤 것을 원하니?
   → _____ do you want, salad _____ soup?

4. Danny와 John 중에서 누가 너의 친구니?
   → _____ is your friend, Danny _____ John?

5. 이 책은 너의 것이니, 그녀의 것이니?
   → Is this book yours _____ _____?

6. 그녀는 의사니, 간호사니?
   → _____ she a doctor _____ a nurse?

 famous 유명한　catch 잡다　always 항상　daughter 딸　salad 샐러드　nurse 간호사

A. 다음 괄호 안의 단어를 이용하여 감탄문을 완성하시오.

Words

A. colorful 화려한
   difficult 어려운

1. _____ _____ _____ story it is! (sad)

2. _____ _____ you are! (nice)

3. _____ _____ flowers they are! (colorful)

4. _____ _____ the test was! (difficult)

B. 다음 대화의 빈칸에 알맞은 말을 쓰시오.

B. potato 감자
   pumpkin 호박

1. *A*: _____ go jogging before breakfast.
   B: _____, let's.

2. *A*: Do you like potatoes _____ pumpkins?
   B: I _____ pumpkins.

3. *A*: Helen is sick, _____ she?
   B: _____, she _____. She has to take a rest.

C. 다음 문장을 괄호 안의 지시대로 바꾸시오.

C. move 이사하다
   furniture 가구

1. You take pictures here. (부정명령문으로)
   → _____

2. Sean moved here last month. (부가의문문으로)
   → _____

3. It is very expensive furniture. (what을 이용한 감탄문으로)
   → _____

4. The box is very heavy. (how를 이용한 감탄문으로)
   → _____

D. 다음 우리말과 같은 뜻이 되도록 빈칸에 알맞은 말을 쓰시오.

D. weekend 주말

1. 정말 달콤한 케이크구나!
   → _____ _____ the cake is!

2. Danny는 축구를 좋아하니, 야구를 좋아하니?
   → Does Danny like soccer _____ _____?

3. 그는 이번 주말에 돌아오지 않을 거야, 그렇지?
   → He won't come back this weekend, _____ _____?

1. 다음 빈칸에 알맞지 <u>않은</u> 것은?

> Don't _____ here.

① run   ② swim
③ eat   ④ sleeps
⑤ play soccer

2. 다음 중 어법상 <u>어색한</u> 것은?

① Please be quiet.
② Let's take not a taxi.
③ What a cute doll it is!
④ She doesn't live in Seoul, does she?
⑤ Which is your ball, this one or that one?

3. 다음 빈칸에 들어갈 말이 나머지와 <u>다른</u> 것은?

① _____ a sunny day it is!
② _____ wonderful the shirt is!
③ _____ sweet strawberries they are!
④ _____ a good friend he is!
⑤ _____ nice pants you have!

4. 다음 우리말을 영어로 바르게 옮긴 것은?

> 그는 정말 정직한 소년이구나!

① What an honest boy he is!
② How an honest boy he is!
③ How honest is the boy!
④ What honest the boy is!
⑤ What honest a boy he is!

5. 다음 중 부가의문문의 쓰임이 <u>잘못된</u> 것은?

① It is a nice gift, isn't it?
② Emma doesn't like a cat, does she?
③ They will go shopping, don't they?
④ Michael can speak Japanese, can't he?
⑤ You didn't call me yesterday, did you?

6. 다음 대화의 빈칸에 알맞은 것은?

> A: Which did you buy, juice or milk?
> B: _____

① Yes, I bought it.
② No, I bought milk.
③ I bought some juice.
④ I bought them at the store.
⑤ I don't like juice.

7. 다음 문장에서 어법상 <u>어색한</u> 것을 찾아 바르게 고치시오.

> Don't drives fast, Dan. It's very dangerous.

_____ → _____

8. 다음 주어진 문장과 뜻이 같도록 빈칸에 알맞은 말을 쓰시오.

> This is a very big city.

= _____ _____ _____ city this is!
= _____ _____ the city is!

9. 다음 빈칸에 알맞은 말이 바르게 짝지어진 것은?

> · _____ quiet in the library.
> · _____ on your gloves.

① Be – Be
② Don't – Put
③ Be – Puts
④ Be – Put
⑤ Being – Be put

10. 다음 빈칸에 알맞은 부가의문문을 쓰시오.

> They are your cookies, _____?

→ _____

11. 다음 중 자연스러운 문장은?

① Don't is worry.
② Let's go fishing.
③ Is careful, Brian.
④ Let's plays the piano.
⑤ Be not listen to the radio.

12. 다음 중 문장의 쓰임이 <u>어색한</u> 것은?

① Don't touch the painting.
② Open the window, please.
③ Don't be late again.
④ Let's swimming in the sea.
⑤ Let's not have lunch together.

13. 다음 문장을 감탄문으로 바르게 옮긴 것은?

> This tower is very beautiful.

① What a beautiful is!
② What a beautiful this!
③ What beautiful this tower is!
④ How beautiful is this tower!
⑤ How beautiful this tower is!

[14-15] 다음 중 어법상 <u>어색한</u> 것을 고르시오.

14. ① Thomas doesn't wear hat, does he?
② You went to the zoo, didn't you?
③ Alice didn't clean the room, did she?
④ Brian can't dance well, won't he?
⑤ Cathy isn't from Canada, is she?

15. ① The boy rode a horse, didn't he?
② Peter likes apples, don't he?
③ She doesn't play the violin, does she?
④ They will go on a picnic, won't they?
⑤ They won't buy the ticket, will they?

16. 다음 대화의 밑줄 친 부분 중 <u>어색한</u> 것은?

> A: You and your brother weren't ① in the park, ② weren't you?
> B: ③ No, we ④ weren't. We ⑤ were at school.

86

to부정사란 무엇인가?
to부정사란 「to+동사원형」의 형태로 문장에서 명사, 형용사, 부사로 쓰이는데, 일정하게 그 쓰임이 정해져 있지 않아서 'to부정사(不定詞)'라고 한다.

동명사란 무엇인가?
동사이지만 명사의 역할을 한다고 해서 동명사라고 하며, 동사 뒤에 -ing를 붙여서 만든다. 동명사는 to부정사의 명사적 용법처럼 명사로 쓰이며 주어, 목적어, 보어 역할을 한다.

Chapter 9. to부정사와 동명사

Unit 24. to부정사 1

Unit 25. to부정사 2

Unit 26. 동명사

24 to부정사 1

1. to부정사의 개념

· to부정사는 「to+동사원형」의 형태로 문장에서 명사, 형용사, 부사의 역할을 한다. 명사로 쓰이면 주어, 목적어, 보어 역할을 하고 형용사로 쓰이면 명사나 대명사 뒤에서 명사나 대명사를 수식한다. 또한 부사로 쓰이면 동사나 형용사를 수식한다.

I like **to watch** movies. 나는 영화 보는 것을 좋아한다. (명사 역할)

I want some milk **to drink**. 나는 마실 우유를 좀 원한다. (형용사 역할)

I go to the store **to buy** clothes. 나는 옷을 사기 위해 그 가게에 간다. (부사 역할)

Check 1 다음 문장에서 to부정사를 찾아 밑줄을 그으시오.

1. They like to read books.

2. To make cookies is very fun.

3. My hobby is to play the violin.

2. to부정사의 명사적 용법

· 문장에서 명사 역할로 주어, 목적어, 보어로 쓰이며 '~하기, ~하는 것'으로 해석한다.

(1) 주어 : to부정사가 주어의 자리에 와서 '~하는 것은'이라고 해석한다.

To play soccer is fun. 축구를 하는 것은 재미있다.

To speak English is not easy. 영어를 말하는 것은 쉽지 않다.

(= It is not easy **to speak** English.)

＊to부정사가 주어로 사용되는 경우에는 가주어 it을 사용하여 to부정사를 뒤로 이동할 수 있다.

(2) 목적어 : to부정사가 목적어의 자리에 와서 '~하는 것을'이라고 해석한다.

I want **to eat** some bread. 나는 약간의 빵을 먹기를 원한다.

I like **to take** a walk after dinner. 나는 저녁 식사 후에 산책하는 것을 좋아한다.

(3) 보어 : to부정사가 보어의 자리에 와서 '~하는 것이다'라고 해석한다.

My dream is **to be** a singer. 나의 꿈은 가수가 되는 것이다.

His plan is **to travel** around the world. 그의 계획은 세계 여행을 하는 것이다.

Check 2 다음 밑줄 친 부분을 우리말로 옮기시오.

1. To play the piano is interesting.

2. We want to meet the man.

3. My hobby is to reading books.

다음 밑줄 친 부분이 주어, 목적어, 보어 중 어떤 역할인지 고르시오.

1. My dream is <u>to be</u> a dentist.　　　　　(주어 / 목적어 / 보어)
2. I like <u>to watch</u> movies.　　　　　　　(주어 / 목적어 / 보어)
3. She decided <u>to buy</u> a new car.　　　　(주어 / 목적어 / 보어)
4. <u>To drive</u> at night is very dangerous.　(주어 / 목적어 / 보어)
5. My hobby is <u>to write</u> novels.　　　　　(주어 / 목적어 / 보어)
6. He wants <u>to drink</u> cold water.　　　　(주어 / 목적어 / 보어)
7. Their hope is <u>to be</u> healthy.　　　　　(주어 / 목적어 / 보어)

Practice 2　다음 문장에서 <u>틀린</u> 곳을 찾아 바르게 고치시오.

1. To swims is good for your health.　　　→ _____
2. My wish is get a new cell phone.　　　→ _____
3. Thomas plans travels to China.　　　　→ _____
4. She wants to meets him again.　　　　→ _____
5. I don't like to went jogging in the morning.　→ _____
6. We love to singing songs together.　　→ _____
7. To keeping a diary every day is difficult.　→ _____

Practice 3　다음 우리말과 같도록 괄호 안의 단어들을 이용하여 문장을 완성하시오.

1. 나는 야채 먹는 것을 좋아하지 않는다. (like, eat)
  = I don't _____ vegetables.

2. 그들은 이번 주말에 소풍을 가기로 결정했다. (decide, go on a picnic)
  = They _____ this weekend.

3. 그녀의 취미는 자전거를 타는 것이다. (be, ride)
  = Her hobby _____ a bike.

4. 아침에 일찍 일어나는 것은 쉽지 않다. (get up, early)
  = _____ in the morning is not easy.

5. 그들은 치즈 케이크를 만들기 시작했다. (begin, make)
  = They _____ a cheese cake.

6. 나는 점심으로 스파게티를 먹기를 원한다. (want, have)
  = I _____ spaghetti for lunch.

Words　dream 꿈　　dentist 치과 의사　　hobby 취미　　novel 소설　　health 건강　　diary 일기

25 | to부정사 2

1. to부정사의 형용사적 용법

· 명사(구)나 대명사의 뒤에서 명사, 대명사를 수식하며 '~할, ~하는'이라고 해석한다.

I have <u>a lot of things</u> <u>to do</u> today. 나는 오늘 해야 할 일이 많다.
　　　　　명사＋to부정사

It's <u>time</u> <u>to go</u> home. 집에 갈 시간이다.
　　　명사＋to부정사

· to부정사의 수식을 받는 명사가 전치사의 목적어인 경우, to부정사 뒤에 있는 전치사를 생략해서는 안 된다.

They look for a house **to live in**. → live in a house 그들은 살 집을 구하고 있다.

Check 1 다음 밑줄 친 to부정사가 수식하는 것을 찾아 동그라미 하시오.

1. Please give me something <u>to drink</u>.

2. I will buy a dress <u>to wear</u> at the party.

3. She has comic books <u>to read</u>.

2. to부정사의 부사적 용법

· 동사나 형용사 등을 수식하여 목적, 감정의 원인, 결과 등을 나타낸다.

(1) 목적 : 주로 동사를 수식하며 '~하기 위해, ~하려고'로 해석한다.

I studied hard **to pass** the test. 나는 시험에 통과하기 위해 열심히 공부했다.

He saved the money **to buy** a bike. 그는 자전거를 사기 위해 돈을 모았다.

(2) 감정의 원인 : 주로 형용사를 수식하며 '~해서, ~하여'로 해석한다.

I'm very glad **to see** you again. 너를 다시 보게 되어 매우 기쁘다.

They were sad **to hear** the news. 그들은 그 소식을 듣게 되어 슬펐다.

감정을 나타내는 형용사	glad, happy, pleased, sad, angry, upset, surprised 등

(3) 결과 : grow up, live 등의 동사 뒤에 와서 '~해서 ~하였다'라고 해석한다.

Harry grew up **to be** a doctor. Harry는 자라서 의사가 되었다.

My grandmother lived **to be** 90 years old. 나의 할머니는 90세까지 사셨다.

Check 2 다음 밑줄 친 부분을 우리말로 옮기시오.

1. I was very happy <u>to pass the test</u>.

2. Lucy grew up <u>to be a cook</u>.

3. I went to the park <u>to meet Jim</u>.

Practice 1 　다음 우리말과 같도록 빈칸에 알맞은 말을 쓰시오.

1. 마실 게 있나요? = Do you have something _____?

2. 그는 앉을 의자를 필요로 했다. = He needed a chair _____ on.

3. 나는 그것에 대해 생각할 시간이 필요하다. = I need some time _____ about it.

4. 그 남자는 자동차를 살 돈을 가지고 있다. = The man has money _____ a car.

5. 우리는 읽을 그 신문을 샀다. = We bought the newspaper _____.

6. 그녀는 쓸 펜을 원한다. = She wants a pen _____ with.

7. 점심 먹을 시간이다. = It's time _____ lunch.

Practice 2 　다음 밑줄 친 부분을 바르게 해석하시오.

1. William was sad to hear the news.　→　_____

2. They came to the park to exercise.　→　_____

3. I'll go to Paris to study art.　→　_____

4. The woman lived to be 95 years old.　→　_____

5. Sophie grew up to be a writer.　→　_____

6. I went to the market to buy bananas.　→　_____

7. I'm happy to meet you again.　→　_____

Practice 3 　다음 우리말과 같도록 단어들을 바르게 배열하여 완성하시오.

1. 그녀는 숨을 장소를 발견했다.

   (found / she / a place / hide in / to)

   → _____

2. 우리는 그를 보고 매우 놀랐다.

   (were / so / see / him / to / we / surprised)

   → _____

3. Tom은 책을 사기 위해 서점에 갔다.

   (books / Tom / to a bookstore / went / to / buy)

   → _____

4. 마실 물이 없었다.

   (no / to / there / water / drink / was)

   → _____

Words　something 무언가　hear 듣다　grow up 자라다　writer 작가　place 장소　hide 숨다

26 동명사

1. 동명사의 개념과 쓰임

• 동명사는 「동사원형+-ing」의 형태로 '~하기, ~하는 것'으로 해석하며 문장에서 명사 역할로 주어, 목적어, 보어로 쓰인다.

(1) 주어 : ~하는 것은

Watching movies is my hobby. 영화 감상은 나의 취미이다.

Doing your best is very important. 최선을 다하는 것은 매우 중요하다.

(2) 목적어 : ~하는 것을

I enjoy **cooking** for my family. 나는 가족을 위해 요리하는 것을 즐긴다.

Susie likes **meeting** new people. Susie는 새로운 사람들을 만나는 것을 좋아한다.

＊전치사 뒤에는 명사나 대명사가 오며 동사가 올 때는 동명사의 형태로 쓴다.

Thank you for **helping** me. 도와줘서 고마워.

(3) 보어 : ~하는 것이다

One of my hobbies is **playing** the piano. 내 취미 중 하나는 피아노를 연주하는 것이다.

Wendy's job is **selling** cars. Wendy의 직업은 자동차를 판매하는 것이다.

Check 1 다음 밑줄 친 부분이 어떤 역할인지 고르시오.

1. Driving fast is very dangerous. (주어 / 목적어 / 보어)

2. My dream is writing novels. (주어 / 목적어 / 보어)

3. My brother hates taking a shower. (주어 / 목적어 / 보어)

---

2. 동사의 목적어 형태

• 동사의 종류에 따라 동명사만을 목적어로 취하거나 to부정사만을 목적어로 취한다.

(1) 동명사만을 목적어로 취하는 동사 : enjoy, finish, avoid, give up, mind keep 등

I finished **doing** my homework. 나는 숙제 하는 것을 끝냈다.

(2) to부정사만을 목적어로 취하는 동사 : want, wish, hope, decide, plan, learn, expect 등

He hopes **to see** Jane again. 그는 Jane을 다시 만나기를 바란다.

(3) 동명사와 to부정사를 모두 목적어로 취하는 동사 : like, love, hate, start, begin 등

The child began **crying**. = The child began **to cry**. 그 어린이는 울기 시작했다.

Check 2 다음 괄호 안에서 알맞은 것을 고르시오.

1. I like (watch / watching) TV show programs.

2. Ann avoids (drinking / to drink) tea in the evening.

3. Kate wants (reading / to read) many books.

Practice 1 다음 괄호 안에서 알맞은 것을 고르시오.

1. My hobby is (play / playing) soccer with friends.

2. Thank you for (come / coming) here.

3. We decided (to take / taking) a taxi home.

4. They planned (to see / seeing) the funny movie.

5. Tony gave up (take / taking) the math test.

6. I hope (eating / to eat) the delicious food.

7. We enjoy (listen / listening) to music.

Practice 2 다음 괄호 안의 단어를 알맞은 형태로 바꿔 쓰시오.

1. Eric and Judy finished _____ the dishes. (do)

2. They expected _____ a movie. (watch)

3. He avoided _____ our questions. (answer)

4. The people planned _____ in winter. (travel)

5. We learned _____ a computer. (use)

6. I gave up _____ the small key. (find)

7. She kept _____ when I was talking. (work)

Practice 3 다음 두 문장이 같도록 빈칸에 알맞은 말을 쓰시오.

1. I hate to get up late. = I hate _____ up late.

2. She began to laugh. = She began _____.

3. I love eating these cookies. = I love to _____ these cookies.

4. They like to watch TV all day. = They like _____ TV all day.

5. Peter started drawing pictures. = Peter started to _____ pictures.

6. Her hobby is reading books. = Her hobby is to _____ books.

7. Riding a horse is very exciting. = To _____ a horse is very exciting.

 Words funny 웃긴, 우스운   give up 포기하다   expect 기대하다   avoid 피하다   answer 답하다   ride 타다

A. 다음 괄호 안의 단어를 알맞은 형태로 바꿔 쓰시오.

1. Helena wants _____ her old friends. (meet)

2. I'm interested in _____. (cook)

3. He enjoyed _____ last winter. (go skiing)

4. They planned _____ a new house. (build)

B. 다음 빈칸에 알맞은 말을 〈보기〉에서 골라 그 기호를 쓰시오.

| 〈보기〉 | ⓐ washing his car | ⓑ to become a great player |
| | ⓒ to hear the news | ⓓ breaking your vase |

1. Susan was surprised _____.

2. I'm sorry for _____.

3. The boy grew up _____.

4. My dad finished _____.

C. 다음 문장에서 어법상 어색한 부분을 바르게 고치시오.

1. I hope seeing you again.　　　　　　→ _____

2. He was glad to got a letter from Jane.　→ _____

3. Monica thinks of to change her mind.　→ _____

4. I got up early taking a walk.　　　　　→ _____

D. 다음 우리말과 같도록 괄호 안의 단어를 이용하여 문장을 완성하시오.

1. 나는 지갑을 잃어버려 슬펐다. (lose, my wallet)

→ I was sad _____.

2. 헤어질 시간이다. (say, goodbye)

→ It is time _____.

3. 그녀는 여기에 머물 시간이 없다. (stay, here)

→ She doesn't have time _____.

4. 나의 여동생은 잡지 읽는 것을 즐긴다. (read, magazines)

→ My sister enjoys _____.

1. 다음 빈칸에 알맞은 것은?

> Do you decide _____ a bike?

① ride   ② to ride
③ riding   ④ to riding
⑤ went riding

2. 다음 밑줄 친 부분을 바르게 고친 것은?

> Jimmy went to the store <u>buy</u> a toy.

① buys   ② bought
③ buying   ④ to buy
⑤ will buy

3. 다음 빈칸에 들어갈 말이 바르게 짝지어진 것은?

> · I hope _____ Canada someday.
> · I'm worried about _____ a test.

① visit – take   ② visiting – taking
③ to visit – taking   ④ visiting – to visit
⑤ to visit – take

4. 다음 중 어법상 옳은 것은?
① I expected going shopping.
② She gave up to study math.
③ He planned going to the zoo this Sunday.
④ My brother is good at speak English.
⑤ They like playing baseball there.

5. 다음 밑줄 친 부분의 용법이 〈보기〉와 같은 것은?

> 〈보기〉 I'm looking for something <u>to drink</u>.

① I begin <u>to watch</u> TV at home.
② My sister has many books <u>to read</u>.
③ She got up early <u>to go</u> jogging.
④ His job is <u>to teach</u> math at school.
⑤ He wants <u>to be</u> an actor.

6. 다음 우리말과 같도록 괄호 안의 단어를 이용하여 문장을 완성하시오.

> 나의 개는 목욕하는 것을 즐긴다.
> (enjoy, take a bath)

→ _____

7. 다음 밑줄 친 to의 쓰임이 나머지와 다른 것은?
① I want <u>to</u> go to the movies.
② Charlie saved the money <u>to</u> buy a bag.
③ Julia went <u>to</u> the park in the morning.
④ Max needs some paper <u>to</u> write on.
⑤ She was surprised <u>to</u> meet him there.

8. 다음 밑줄 친 ①~⑤ 중 어법상 어색한 것은?

> A: Sally, ①<u>did</u> you finish ②<u>to clean</u> your room?
> B: ③<u>Not yet</u>. But I ④<u>will</u> ⑤<u>finish</u> it before lunch.

9. 다음 빈칸에 playing이 들어갈 수 <u>없는</u> 것은?

① We started _____ soccer.

② Jim's hobby is _____ basketball.

③ Susie avoids _____ the piano at night.

④ Thomas learned _____ the cello.

⑤ The baby likes _____ with a ball.

10. 다음 중 어법상 <u>어색한</u> 것은?

① It's time to have lunch.

② Ryan grew up being a police officer.

③ My brother enjoys going fishing.

④ I'm interested in swimming.

⑤ We talked about having a party for Jane.

11. 다음 빈칸에 알맞은 동사의 형태는?

> Thank you for _____ me.

① call ② calls

③ calling ④ to call

⑤ called

12. 다음 두 문장이 같도록 빈칸에 알맞은 것은?

> To exercise regularly is very hard.
> = _____ is very hard to exercise regularly.

① It ② That

③ This ④ Those

⑤ They

[13-14] 다음 중 빈칸에 들어갈 수 <u>없는</u> 것을 고르시오.

13.
> Julia _____ to learn to drive a car.

① kept ② planned

③ hoped ④ decided

⑤ began

14.
> Brian _____ washing his car.

① enjoyed ② finished

③ wanted ④ gave up

⑤ stopped

15. 다음 중 동명사의 역할이 나머지와 <u>다른</u> 것은?

① He likes talking with others.

② I stopped watching TV.

③ He finished writing a letter.

④ How about going out to eat?

⑤ Sending an e-mail is easy.

16. 다음 중 동명사의 역할이 〈보기〉와 같은 것은?

> 〈보기〉 My hobby is taking pictures.

① Playing golf is very boring.

② Learning English is fun.

③ I can't stop laughing.

④ My job is selling computers.

⑤ Brian gave up taking the test.

문장의 요소는 무엇인가?

문장의 주요소는 문장을 구성하는 데 반드시 있어야 하는 것으로 주어, 동사, 목적어, 보어가 있다. 수식요소는 주어, 동사, 목적어, 보어를 뺀 나머지이며 주요소를 꾸미는 역할을 한다. 문장에서 주요소의 구성에 따라 1~5형식으로 문장을 구분한다.

1형식 : 「주어+동사」로 이루어진 문장
2형식 : 「주어+동사+보어」로 이루어진 문장
3형식 : 「주어+동사+목적어」로 이루어진 문장
4형식 : 「주어+동사+간접목적어+직접목적어」로 이루어진 문장
5형식 : 「주어+동사+목적어+목적격보어」로 이루어진 문장

Chapter 10. 문장의 형태

27 | There is/are, 감각동사

1. There is, There are

· There is와 There are는 '~이 있다'라는 뜻으로 There is 뒤에는 단수명사가, There are 뒤에는 복수명사가 온다.

긍정문	There is+단수명사 ~. There are+복수명사 ~.	**There is** a book on the table. 탁자 위에 책이 있다. **There is** some milk in the bottle. 병 안에 우유가 좀 있다. **There are** some oranges in the basket. 바구니에 오렌지가 좀 있다. ＊셀 수 없는 명사는 단수 취급하므로 There is ~.로 쓴다.
부정문	There is[are]+not ~.	**There isn't** much money in my purse. 내 지갑에 돈이 많이 없다. **There aren't** any pencils on the desk. 책상 위에 연필이 없다.
의문문	Is[Are] there ~? – Yes, there is[are]. – No, there isn't[aren't].	**Is there** a bank near here? 은행이 여기 근처에 있나요? – Yes, there is. / No, there isn't. **Are there** any students in the classroom? 교실에 학생들이 있나요? – Yes, there are. / No, there aren't.

Check 1 다음 빈칸에 알맞은 말을 쓰시오.

1. There _____ a lot of sugar in the jar.
2. There _____ many balls in the room.
3. _____ there a station near here?

2. 감각동사+형용사

· look, sound, feel, smell, taste 등과 같이 사람의 감각을 표현하는 동사를 감각동사라고 한다. 감각동사 뒤에는 주격보어로 형용사가 오는데 부사처럼 해석한다.

＊주격보어는 주어의 상태나 성질을 설명하는 역할을 한다.

look(~하게 보이다)	He **looks** happy today. 그는 오늘 행복하게 보인다.
sound(~하게 들리다)	Her voice **sounds** sweet. 그녀의 목소리는 달콤하게 들린다.
feel(~하게 느끼다)	I **feel** hungry. 나는 허기를 느낀다.
smell(~한 냄새가 나다)	This soup **smells** good. 이 수프는 좋은 냄새가 난다.
taste(~한 맛이 나다)	The pizza **tasted** salty. 그 피자는 짠맛이 났다.

Check 2 다음 괄호 안에서 알맞은 것을 고르시오.

1. This silk feels (soft / softly).
2. You look very (angry / angrily).
3. This coffee tastes (sweet / sweetly).

다음 괄호 안에서 알맞은 것을 골라 빈칸에 쓰시오.

1. There _____ chairs in the room. (is, are)

2. There _____ a cat under the tree. (is, are)

3. There _____ any books in my bag. (isn't, aren't)

4. There _____ some juice in the glass. (is, are)

5. There _____ any cheese in the kitchen. (isn't, aren't)

6. There _____ any ducks on the pond. (isn't, aren't)

7. There _____ many things in this shop. (is, are)

Practice 2 다음 빈칸에 알맞은 말을 넣어 대화를 완성하시오.

1. _____ any milk in the refrigerator?   – Yes, there is.

2. _____ any umbrellas on the desk?   – No, there aren't.

3. _____ many birds in the sky?   – Yes, _____ .

4. _____ a bookstore at the corner?   – No, _____ .

5. _____ much juice in the bottle?   – No, _____ .

6. _____ a ball on the ground?   – Yes, _____ .

7. _____ three rooms in the house?   – Yes, _____ .

Practice 3 다음 우리말과 같도록 빈칸에 알맞은 말을 쓰시오.

1. 그는 피곤해 보인다. = He _____ tired.

2. 이 빵은 좋은 냄새가 난다. = This bread _____ good.

3. 그녀의 노래는 슬프게 들린다. = Her song _____ sad.

4. 그 소년은 친절해 보인다. = The boy _____ kind.

5. 이 블라우스는 부드러운 느낌이 난다. = This blouse _____ soft.

6. 사과는 단맛이 난다. = Apples _____ sweet.

7. 그들은 행복하게 느껴졌다. = They _____ happy.

Words pond 연못   thing 물건   refrigerator 냉장고   corner 모퉁이   ground 땅, 운동장   soft 부드러운

28 4형식 문장과 수여동사

1. 수여동사

· 4형식 문장에는 수여동사가 쓰이는데 수여동사는 두 개의 목적어를 가지는 동사로 '~에게 ~을 주다'라는 뜻이다. 수여동사에는 give, send, teach, bring, buy, make, show, teach, tell, cook, write 등이 있다.

My father **gave** <u>me</u> <u>a camera</u>. 나의 아버지는 나에게 카메라를 주셨다.
              간접목적어 직접목적어

Nick **made** <u>us</u> <u>sweet cookies</u>. Nick은 우리에게 달콤한 과자를 만들어 주었다.
           간접목적어   직접목적어

＊문장의 형식

1형식 문장(주어+동사)	The birds sing. 그 새들이 노래한다.
2형식 문장(주어+동사+보어)	He is a good singer. 그는 좋은 가수이다.
3형식 문장(주어+동사+목적어)	Brian meets Lisa. Brian은 Lisa를 만난다.
4형식 문장(주어+동사+간접목적어+직접목적어)	She gives me a doll. 그녀는 나에게 인형을 준다.
5형식 문장(주어+동사+목적어+목적격보어)	They make him happy. 그들은 그를 행복하게 만든다.

> **Check 1** 다음 문장에서 해당 요소를 찾아 동그라미 하시오.
> 1. He told me an exciting story. (간접목적어)
> 2. I gave Jim a pencil. (수여동사)
> 3. My mother cooks me pizza. (직접목적어)

2. 수여동사 문장의 전환

· 간접목적어와 직접목적어의 자리를 바꾸어 4형식 문장을 3형식 문장으로 전환할 수 있다. 간접목적어와 직접목적어의 자리를 바꾸고 뒤로 이동한 간접목적어 앞에 전치사를 붙이는데 이때, 전치사는 동사에 따라 달라진다.

He gave me a flower. → He gave a flower <u>to me</u>. 그는 나에게 꽃을 주었다.

She bought me a new hat. → She bought a new hat <u>for me</u>.
그녀는 나에게 새 모자를 사주었다.

They asked me many questions. → They asked many questions <u>of me</u>.
그들은 나에게 많은 질문들을 했다.

to가 필요한 동사	bring, give, lend, send, show, teach, tell, write 등
for가 필요한 동사	buy, cook, find, get, make 등
of가 필요한 동사	ask 등

> **Check 2** 다음 괄호 안에서 알맞은 것을 고르시오.
> 1. Max sent a letter (to / for) his friend.
> 2. They will buy a tie (for / of) their father.
> 3. I asked a question (to / of) Ann.

1. (me, questions, he, asked) → _____
2. (made, she, pizza, us) → _____
3. (him, a story, Emily, told) → _____
4. (gave, pencils, them, he) → _____
5. (will, I, my room, you, show) → _____
6. (us, Ann, erasers, bought) → _____
7. (a letter, Jim, wrote, her) → _____

1. They asked some questions (to / for / of) him.
2. I will send some books (to / for / of) Amy.
3. She is teaching English (to / for / of) students.
4. My mother made an apple pie (to / for / of) me.
5. His uncle bought a new bike (to / for / of) him.
6. She will tell the truth (to / for / of) you.
7. They showed their albums (to / for / of) Helen.

1. David gave him a birthday present.
   → _____

2. We made Lisa a big chocolate cake.
   → _____

3. Daniel bought his mom a yellow scarf.
   → _____

4. My sister asked me a strange question.
   → _____

5. Mr. Johnson taught them history.
   → _____

6. My aunt cooked her daughter spaghetti.
   → _____

Words question 질문   letter 편지   truth 진실   album 사진첩, 앨범   present 선물   strange 이상한

29 | 5형식 문장과 목적격보어

1. 목적격보어 – 명사/형용사

• 5형식 문장은 「주어+동사+목적어+목적격보어」로 구성된 문장으로, 목적격보어에는 명사나 형용사, to부정사 등이 올 수 있다. 5형식 문장에서 명사나 형용사를 목적격보어로 사용하는 동사는 make, call, name, keep, find 등이다.

They **named** their baby Tony. 그들은 그들의 아기를 Tony라고 이름 지었다.
　　　　　　목적어　　목적격보어(명사)

The news **made** me happy. 그 소식은 나를 행복하게 만들었다.
　　　　　　목적어　목적격보어(형용사)

I **found** his novel interesting. 나는 그의 소설이 흥미롭다는 것을 알았다.
　　　　목적어　　　목적격보어(형용사)

* 목적격보어는 목적어를 보충 설명해 주는 말로 목적어의 성격이나 상태, 성질 등을 나타낸다.

> **Check 1** 다음 문장에서 목적격보어를 찾아 동그라미 하시오.
>
> 1. An air conditioner keeps you cool.
> 2. She made me upset.
> 3. He called his dog Joe.

2. 목적격보어 – to부정사

• 5형식 문장의 목적격보어에는 to부정사가 올 수도 있는데, 이 경우에는 목적어의 행동을 설명해 준다. to부정사를 목적격보어로 사용하는 동사는 want, tell, ask, allow, advise, expect 등이다.

I **want** you **to go** with me. 나는 네가 나와 함께 가기를 원한다.
　　　목적어 목적격보어(to부정사)

He **advised** me **to exercise** every day. 그는 내게 매일 운동하라고 조언했다.
　　　　　목적어 목적격보어(to부정사)

목적격보어에 명사나 형용사가 오는 동사	make, call, name, keep, find 등
목적격보어에 to부정사가 오는 동사	want, tell, ask, allow, advise, expect 등

> **Check 2** 다음 괄호 안에서 알맞은 것을 고르시오.
>
> 1. He asked me (help / to help) with his work.
> 2. My mother told me (cleans / to clean) my room.
> 3. I want you (come / to come) to my party.

다음 우리말과 같도록 빈칸에 알맞은 말을 쓰시오.

1. 그녀는 그를 Luke라고 불렀다.
   = She called _____ Luke.

2. 그 음악은 나를 행복하게 만들었다.
   = The music made me _____.

3. 이 스웨터는 너를 따뜻하게 유지해 줄 것이다.
   = This sweater will keep you _____.

4. 그녀는 그 영화가 지루하다는 것을 알았다.
   = She found the movie _____.

5. 그들은 그 아기를 Susan이라고 이름 지었다.
   = They named the _____ Susan.

6. 그는 그의 아들을 의사로 만들었다.
   = He _____ his son a doctor.

7. 수영은 너를 건강하게 유지시킨다.
   = Swimming keeps you _____.

다음 괄호 안의 단어를 알맞은 형태로 바꿔 빈칸에 쓰시오.

1. My mom asked me _____ her. (help)

2. He told them _____ tonight. (call)

3. She allowed him _____ her computer. (use)

4. They wanted me _____ with them. (go)

5. The teacher advised students _____ hard. (study)

6. Bob expected Nancy _____ his team. (join)

7. He advised his son _____ carefully. (drive)

다음 괄호 안의 단어들을 바르게 배열하여 문장을 완성하시오.

1. It will keep _____. (safe, you)

2. I found _____. (empty, the box)

3. She allowed _____. (to, go out, her son)

4. They told _____. (get up, her, to, early)

5. Judy wanted _____. (me, her house, to, visit)

6. The doctor advised _____. (eat, to, him, vegetables)

7. I asked _____. (my friend, take, pictures, to)

Words warm 따뜻한 boring 지루한 son 아들 allow 허락하다 expect 기대하다 advise 충고하다 empty 빈

103

A. 다음 밑줄 친 부분의 문장 요소가 무엇인지 〈보기〉에서 골라 쓰시오.

〈보기〉 간접목적어   직접목적어   주격보어   목적격보어

1. Karen sent <u>Laura</u> a small gift.

2. Joseph looked <u>worried</u>.

3. She bought me <u>a new laptop</u>.

4. My mother advised me <u>to have breakfast</u>.

B. 다음 괄호 안에서 알맞은 것을 고르시오.

1. Kate wants me (go / to go) shopping with her.

2. Will you find socks (for / to) me?

3. This soup smells (good / well).

4. (Is / Are) there any pepper in the store?

C. 다음 우리말과 같도록 괄호 안의 단어를 이용하여 문장을 완성하시오.

1. 이 케이크는 형편없는 맛이 난다. (terrible)

   → This cake _____ _____.

2. 하늘에 많은 연들이 있다. (many kites)

   → _____ _____ _____ _____ in the sky.

3. 그는 나에게 피자를 만들어 주었다. (made, pizza, for)

   → He _____ _____ _____ _____.

D. 다음 문장에서 어법상 어색한 곳을 찾아 밑줄 긋고 바르게 고치시오.

1. Our math teacher told us study hard.   → _____

2. There aren't much jam in the bottle.   → _____

3. Carol felt tiredly, so she took a rest at home. → _____

4. The man gave a nice ring for the woman.   → _____

1. 다음 빈칸에 알맞지 <u>않은</u> 것은?

> There are _____ in the room.

① three beds   ② many children
③ some books   ④ my pants
⑤ lots of paper

2. 다음 중 어법상 옳은 것은?
   ① Tommy felt very sadly.
   ② The bread smelled well.
   ③ Her voice sounds sweetly.
   ④ Your dress looks wonderful.
   ⑤ This pie tastes nicely.

3. 다음 빈칸에 공통으로 알맞은 말을 쓰시오.

> · He taught Japanese _____ me.
> · She showed her pictures _____ us.

→ _____

4. 다음 빈칸에 들어갈 말이 바르게 짝지어진 것은?

> · May I ask a favor _____ you?
> · He made a toy car _____ his son.

① of – to   ② of – for
③ to – to   ④ for – for
⑤ to – of

5. 다음 대화의 빈칸에 알맞은 것은?

> A: Is there a bakery near your house?
> B: _____

① Yes, there is.   ② Yes, there are.
③ No, there aren't.   ④ No, it isn't.
⑤ Yes, there isn't.

6. 다음 두 문장이 같도록 빈칸에 들어갈 말이 바르게 짝지어진 것은?

> I watched the movie. It was very funny.
> = I _____ the movie very _____.

① found – fun   ② found – funny
③ watched – funny   ④ watched – fun
⑤ told – funny

7. 다음 빈칸에 들어갈 말이 나머지와 <u>다른</u> 것은?
   ① Tom told a sad story _____ me.
   ② My mother cooked lunch _____ me.
   ③ She wrote a letter _____ her teacher.
   ④ I will show some photos _____ you.
   ⑤ They gave a big ball _____ Sarah.

8. 다음 빈칸에 알맞은 것은?

> This coat will _____.

① keep you warm   ② keep you warmly
③ keep warm you   ④ keep warmly
⑤ you to keep warm

[9-10] 다음 문장의 빈칸에 알맞은 것을 고르시오.

9.

He bought a gift _____ his wife.

① of
② to
③ in
④ for
⑤ at

10.

He asks questions _____ them.

① of
② to
③ for
④ from
⑤ in

11. 다음 중 어법상 어색한 것은?

① He found the book difficult.
② We call the baby Jake.
③ I want you to have dinner with me.
④ His music made us comfortable.
⑤ Linda allowed him watching TV.

12. 다음 글의 밑줄 친 ①~⑤ 중 어법상 어색한 곳을 찾아 바르게 고치시오.

We ①were taking a walk in the park ②yesterday. Two girls ③came to us and they ④asked us ⑤take a picture.

_____ → _____

[13-14] 다음 〈보기〉와 문장의 형식이 같은 것을 고르시오.

13.

〈보기〉 The shop begins at nine o'clock.

① They run very fast.
② The boy is sad.
③ She likes grapes.
④ She was sick last night.
⑤ A man opens the window.

14.

〈보기〉 The child looks happy.

① They study hard.
② We play baseball.
③ He is a teacher.
④ I teach them science.
⑤ The birds fly in the sky.

15. 다음 중 문장의 형식이 나머지와 다른 것은?

① She knows him.
② I watch TV all day.
③ He meets the people.
④ Amy likes her new school.
⑤ The girl became the actress.

16. 다음 중 자연스러운 문장은?

① We are closely friends.
② He wants you to go there.
③ I write to her an e-mail.
④ Give the chair me, please.
⑤ This food tastes very well.

전치사는 무엇인가?

전치사는 명사 앞에서 장소나 방향, 시간 등을 명확하게 알려주는 역할을 한다. 전치사는 역할에 따라 알맞은 전치사를 사용해야 하며 명사나 대명사와 함께 쓴다.

전치사에는 어떤 것이 있는가?

전치사는 명사와 함께 쓰여 시간, 장소, 위치, 방향, 방법 등을 나타내 주고, 그 외에도 다양한 전치사가 있다.

Chapter 11. 전치사

30 시간의 전치사

1. at, on, in

· 전치사는 명사나 대명사 앞에 쓰여 시간, 장소, 위치, 방향, 수단, 목적 등을 나타내는 역할을 한다. 시간의 전치사에는 at, on, in 등이 있다.

at	구체적인 시각, 특정한 시점(정오, 자정, 밤)	at 10:30, at night, at noon, at that time, … I usually get up at 6:30. Don't stay up late at night.
on	요일, 날짜, 특정한 날	on Sunday, on July 8th, on Christmas Day, … Let's go hiking on Saturday morning. What are you going to do on Christmas eve?
in	오전, 오후, 저녁, 연도, 월, 계절	in the afternoon, in 2013, in March, in summer, … My father reads the newspaper in the morning. It is too hot in August.

> **Check 1** 다음 빈칸에 at, on, in 중 알맞은 것을 쓰시오.
>
> 1. _____ night
> 2. _____ winter
> 3. _____ New Year's Day

2. before, after, for, during

· at, on, in 외에 시간을 나타내는 전치사에는 before, after, for, during이 있다.

before	~ 전에	before breakfast, before 8 o'clock, … I will come back before dinner.
after	~ 후에	after dinner, after the class, … He went to the movies after dinner.
for	~ 동안(+숫자를 포함한 구체적인 기간)	for two hours, for a week, for five years, … Tina stayed in Paris for two weeks.
during	~ 동안(+특정 기간)	during summer vacation, during this weekend, … I will travel to Japan during summer vacation.

> **Check 2** 다음 밑줄 친 부분을 우리말로 옮기시오.
>
> 1. I made a kite <u>for two hours</u>.
> 2. She goes to bed <u>before 10:00</u>.
> 3. It rained a lot <u>during the summer festival</u>.

Practice 1 다음 빈칸에 at, on, in 중에서 알맞은 것을 쓰시오.

1. The twins were born _____ 2015.
2. I will call her _____ seven p.m.
3. What are you going to do _____ Christmas?
4. I usually go to school _____ 7:30.
5. They go to church _____ Sundays.
6. She will plant trees _____ Arbor Day.

Practice 2 다음 괄호 안에서 알맞은 것을 고르시오.

1. I lived in London (for / during) ten years.
2. Wash your hands (before / during) dinner.
3. She traveled to Paris (in / during) the Christmas holidays.
4. They waited for him (for / during) an hour.
5. James goes to the house (before / for) the sunset.
6. We had a good time (for / during) the field trip.

Practice 3 다음 우리말과 같도록 빈칸에 알맞은 말을 쓰시오.

1. 그는 종종 식사 전에 간식을 먹는다.
   = He often eats snacks _____ meals.

2. 그 야구 경기는 10월 19일에 있다.
   = The baseball game is _____ October 19th.

3. 나는 3시간 동안 치즈 케이크를 만들었다.
   = I made a cheese cake _____ three hours.

4. 그녀는 오후에 도착할 것이다.
   = She will arrive _____ the afternoon.

5. 밤 늦게까지 깨어 있지 마라.
   = Don't stay up late _____ night.

6. 우리는 여름에 항상 해변에 간다.
   = We always go to the beach _____ summer.

7. 그들은 겨울 방학 동안 프랑스에 머물렀다.
   = They stayed in France _____ the winter vacation.

 Words plant 심다   Arbor Day 식목일   holiday 휴일   sunset 일몰   field trip 현장 학습   snack 간식

31 | 장소와 위치의 전치사

1. 장소의 전치사

· 장소를 나타내는 전치사에는 at, in이 있다.

at	비교적 좁은 장소나 지점	at the bus stop, at home, at the corner, ··· I want to watch a movie at home. She saw Andrew at the corner.
in	비교적 넓은 장소	in Seoul, in Korea, in the city, in the world, ··· It snowed heavily in London. My aunt lives in Canada.

> **Check 1 다음 괄호 안에서 알맞은 것을 고르시오.**
> 1. I want to study Art (at / in) Paris.
> 2. China is (at / in) Asia.
> 3. We met the singer (at / in) the bus stop.

2. 위치의 전치사

· 위치를 나타내는 전치사에는 다양한 것이 있다.

in	~ 안에	He is studying in his room.
on	~ 위에(표면에 접한 상태)	There is a picture on the wall.
under	~ 아래에	There are children under the tree.
next to(= by)	~ 옆에	My school is next to the bakery.
in front of	~ 앞에	She stopped in front of the store.
behind	~ 뒤에	A dog is sleeping behind the bench.
over	~ 위에(표면에 접하지 않은 상태)	The plane is flying over the building.
near	~ 근처에	There is a park near my house.
between A and B	A와 B 사이에	I sat between Kate and Andy.
across from	~ 맞은편에	The bank is across from the library.

> **Check 2 다음 우리말과 같도록 빈칸에 알맞은 말을 쓰시오.**
> 1. I found my gloves _____ the sofa. (그 소파 아래에서)
> 2. He is standing _____ the hospital. (그 병원 맞은편에)
> 3. Is there a station _____ here? (여기 근처에)

다음 빈칸에 in 또는 at을 쓰시오.

1. Let's meet _____ the bus stop.
2. They will stay _____ home today.
3. There are many beautiful places _____ the world.
4. We can see lots of stars _____ the sky.
5. She sees John _____ the corner.
6. Kenya is located _____ Africa.

Practice 2　다음 우리말과 같도록 괄호 안에서 알맞은 것을 고르시오.

1. The ducks were floating (on / over) the water. (그 물 위에)

2. He found my cap (in front of / behind) the sofa. (그 소파 뒤에서)

3. The hospital is (near / next to) the post office. (그 우체국 근처에)

4. Some children are standing (by / under) the truck. (그 트럭 옆에)

5. She sat (between / across from) him. (그의 맞은편에)

6. The ball is (in front of / over) the backpack. (그 배낭 앞에)

Practice 3　다음 우리말과 같도록 빈칸에 알맞은 말을 쓰시오.

1. 나의 집 근처에는 공원이 많이 있다.
   = There are many parks _____ my house.

2. 그 호수 옆에는 오래된 집이 한 채 있었다.
   = There was an old house _____ the lake.

3. 나의 남동생은 문 뒤에 숨어 있었다.
   = My brother was hiding _____ the door.

4. 그 식당 맞은편에 은행이 있어요.
   = There is a bank _____ the restaurant.

5. 그는 그의 강아지를 탁자 아래에서 보았다.
   = He saw his puppy _____ the table.

6. 커다란 시계가 벽에 있었다.
   = A big clock was _____ the wall.

7. 나의 여동생은 Sally와 Jane 사이에 있다.
   = My sister is _____ Sally _____ Jane.

Words　place 장소　locate 위치하다　float 떠다니다　post office 우체국　lake 호수　puppy 강아지　clock 시계

Unit 32 다양한 쓰임의 전치사

1. 방향의 전치사

· 전치사는 방향을 나타내기도 하는데, up, down, into, out of 등이 있다.

up	~ 위로	He walked **up** the hill.
down	~ 아래로	The kid came **down** the stairs.
into	~ 안으로	The frog jumped **into** the lake.
out of	~ 밖으로	She came **out of** the house.
from	~로부터	They came **from** Mexico.
to	~로	I'm going **to** the station.
for	~를 향하여	We will leave **for** London tomorrow.

Check 1 다음 밑줄 친 부분을 우리말로 옮기시오.

1. The boy climbed <u>up the tree</u>.
2. A bear went <u>into the woods</u>.
3. The train started <u>for New York</u>.

2. 다양한 전치사

· 전치사는 수단이나 방법 등 다양한 의미를 나타낸다.

by	~을 타고	I go to school **by** bus.
for	~을 위해	This is **for** you.
with	~와 함께, ~을 가지고	He will go camping **with** his friends.
without	~ 없이	We can't live **without** water.
about	~에 대해	I heard the news **about** John.
around	~ 주위에	She will travel **around** the world.

Check 2 다음 괄호 안에서 알맞은 것을 고르시오.

1. I visit my grandparents (by / for) subway.
2. She cut the bread (with / about) a knife.
3. The earth moves (without / around) the sun.

다음 괄호 안에서 알맞은 것을 골라 빈칸에 쓰시오.

1. I heard the news _____ the animal. (about / around)
2. We will play soccer _____ his brother. (by / with)
3. They went to the park _____ subway. (for / by)
4. The child climbed _____ the tree. (up / out of)
5. We can't live _____ water. (without / for)
6. The stone rolled _____ the hill. (down / into)

Practice 2 다음 우리말과 같도록 괄호 안에서 알맞은 것을 고르시오.

1. The airplane leaves (to / for) London. (런던을 향해)
2. A frog jumped (into / out of) the pond. (그 연못 안으로)
3. The workers were climbing (up / down) the ladder. (그 사다리 위로)
4. Pedro came (to / from) Mexico. (멕시코에서)
5. There are lots of snakes (around / into) the woods. (그 숲 주변에)
6. Lisa baked some cookies (without / for) the meeting. (그 모임을 위해)

Practice 3 다음 우리말과 같도록 밑줄 친 부분을 바르게 고치시오.

1. 달은 지구 주위를 돈다.
   = The moon moves <u>to</u> the earth.   → _____
2. 그 선수는 물 속으로 다이빙했다.
   = The player dived <u>out of</u> the water.   → _____
3. 우리는 그녀 없이 거기에 가지 않을 것이다.
   = We won't go there <u>with</u> her.   → _____
4. Sarah는 칼로 빵을 잘랐다.
   = Sarah cut the bread <u>without</u> a knife.   → _____
5. 우리는 도서관으로 가는 중이다.
   = We are going <u>for</u> the library.   → _____
6. 여우가 동굴 밖으로 뛰어 나왔다.
   = A fox ran <u>down</u> the cave.   → _____
7. 이것은 나의 남동생을 위한 것이다.
   = This is <u>from</u> my brother.   → _____

 Words climb 올라가다   roll 굴러가다   worker 노동자   ladder 사다리   dive 다이빙하다   cave 동굴

113

A. 다음 빈칸에 공통으로 알맞은 전치사를 쓰시오.

1. She lived _____ Korea _____ 2012.

2. He landed _____ the moon _____ July 16th.

3. _____ noon, I met Julia _____ the bus stop.

Words

A. land 착륙하다
   moon 달

B. 다음 밑줄 친 부분을 바르게 고치시오.

1. Dean was drawing <u>during</u> two hours. → _____

2. My house is across <u>to</u> the park. → _____

3. Amy comes <u>for</u> Japan. She is Japanese. → _____

4. You should brush your teeth <u>after</u> going to bed. → _____

B. Japan 일본
   brush the teeth 양치질하다

C. 다음 괄호 안에서 알맞은 것을 골라 빈칸에 쓰시오.

1. The ship was passing _____ the bridge. (under / over)

2. He put the ball _____ Judy and Tina. (by / between)

3. Friday comes _____ Thursday. (before / after)

4. Children should not go _____ the fire. (near / across)

C. pass 지나가다
   bridge 다리
   fire 불

D. 다음 우리말과 같도록 괄호 안의 단어를 이용하여 문장을 완성하시오.

1. 나는 월요일부터 금요일까지 수업이 있다. (Monday, Friday)
   → I have classes _____.

2. 그는 빗속에서 우산 없이 걸어갔다. (umbrella)
   → He _____ in the rain.

3. 그녀는 그 여름 방학 동안 여행을 할 것이다. (take a trip)
   → She will _____.

4. 큰 눈덩이가 언덕 아래로 굴러 내려왔다. (roll)
   → A big snowball _____.

D. class 수업
   trip 여행
   snowball 눈덩이

1. 다음 빈칸에 알맞지 <u>않은</u> 것은?

> I saw Jennifer at _____.

① the station   ② five o'clock
③ the concert   ④ noon
⑤ Sunday

2. 다음 중 어법상 어색한 것은?

① She walked around the lake.
② I have a test in April 21st.
③ He wants to go there without her.
④ The dog is barking in front of the door.
⑤ There are many bees over the flowers.

3. 다음 빈칸에 들어갈 말이 바르게 짝지어진 것은?

> · It's warm _____ spring.
> · I got up _____ 7:10 this morning.

① on – at   ② in – at
③ in – on   ④ at – in
⑤ on – in

4. 다음 두 문장이 같도록 빈칸에 알맞은 말을 쓰시오.

> There is a table next to the bed.
> = There is a table _____ the bed.

→ _____

5. 다음 문장에서 어법상 어색한 부분을 찾아 바르게 고치시오.

> There are many people in front to the post office.

_____ → _____

6. 다음 빈칸에 공통으로 알맞은 것은?

> · I live _____ my cousin.
> · The baby is playing _____ a doll.

① with   ② around
③ on   ④ across
⑤ for

7. 다음 빈칸에 들어갈 말이 나머지와 <u>다른</u> 것은?

① There is a mirror _____ the wall.
② The cat is sleeping _____ the floor.
③ We had a great time _____ the festival.
④ I go to church _____ Sundays.
⑤ They eat turkey _____ Thanksgiving Day.

8. 다음 우리말과 같도록 빈칸에 알맞은 말을 쓰시오.

> 나는 곤충에 관한 그 책들을 읽었다.
> = I read the books _____ insects.

→ _____

9. 다음 중 밑줄 친 부분이 어법상 옳은 것은?

① I feel sleepy <u>at</u> spring.

② Jonathan will come back <u>in</u> Tuesday.

③ She drinks tea <u>at</u> the morning.

④ They play badminton <u>on</u> school.

⑤ I cleaned the room <u>for</u> 30 minutes.

10. 다음 빈칸에 during이 올 수 <u>없는</u> 것은?

① I was bored _____ his speech.

② She is running _____ an hour.

③ It rained a lot _____ the night.

④ I had a cup of coffee _____ the break.

⑤ He had a great time _____ the vacation.

[11–12] 다음 빈칸에 우리말에 해당하는 말을 쓰시오.

11.
> Peter and Ann will leave <u>~을 향해</u> Seoul in the evening.

→ _____

12.
> I studied history <u>~ 동안</u> the summer vacation.

→ _____

[13–14] 다음 빈칸에 알맞은 말을 고르시오.

13.
> She went to the museum _____ bus.

① of   ② to

③ at   ④ by

⑤ on

14.
> The school begins _____ nine o'clock.

① at   ② on

③ by   ④ in

⑤ with

15. 다음 빈칸에 들어갈 말이 바르게 짝지어진 것은?

> We work _____ Monday _____ Friday.

① how – to   ② from – in

③ from – to   ④ when – to

⑤ on – from

16. 다음 빈칸에 들어갈 말이 나머지와 <u>다른</u> 것은?

① She was born _____ 2005.

② They are _____ the corner.

③ We go to the sea _____ summer.

④ My dad is _____ the living room.

⑤ We have a Christmas _____ December.

접속사는 무엇인가?
접속사는 단어와 단어, 어구와 어구, 문장과 문장을 연결해 주는
역할을 한다. 문장의 의미에 따라 대등하게 또는 종속적으로 이
어준다.

접속사에는 어떤 것이 있는가?
접속사 중에는 서로 대등한 항목들을 연결하는 접속사(and, but,
or, so)와 문장 앞에서 그 문장을 명사나 부사로 만드는 접속사
(when, before, after, because, that, if)가 있다.

Chapter 12. 접속사

33 | and, but, or, so

1. and

- 서로 대등한 것을 연결해 주는 것을 등위접속사라고 하는데, 등위접속사는 단어와 단어, 구와 구, 절과 절을 연결하는 역할을 한다.
- and는 '~와, 그리고'라는 뜻으로 서로 비슷한 내용을 연결한다. 세 개 이상의 것을 나열할 때는 마지막에 and를 쓴다.

  He has blue eyes **and** brown hair. 그는 파란 눈과 갈색 머리카락을 가지고 있다.

  She watched TV, **and** he listened to music. 그녀는 TV를 봤고 그는 음악을 들었다.

  I bought apples, strawberries, **and** bananas. 나는 사과, 딸기, 그리고 바나나를 샀다.

  *세 개 이상을 연결할 때는 마지막에 and를 넣어서 표현한다.

2. but

- but은 '그러나, 하지만'이라는 뜻으로 서로 반대되는 내용을 연결한다.

  He is young **but** very brave. 그는 어리지만 매우 용감하다.

  My mother is not a nurse **but** a teacher. 나의 어머니는 간호사가 아니고 선생님이다.

  It was very sunny yesterday, **but** I stayed at home. 어제는 매우 맑았지만 나는 집에 있었다.

Check 1 다음 괄호 안에서 알맞은 것을 고르시오.

1. I ate a sandwich (and / but) salad for lunch.
2. She likes to sing (and / but) dance.
3. Penguins have swings, (and / but) they can't fly.

---

3. or

- or은 '~이거나, 또는'이라는 뜻으로 둘 중 하나를 선택하여 말할 때 쓴다.

  You can have pizza **or** spaghetti. 당신은 피자 또는 스파게티를 먹을 수 있다.

  Which do you like better, coffee **or** tea? 커피와 차 중에서 어느 것을 더 좋아하나요?

  Let's meet at twelve **or** at one. 12시나 1시에 만나자.

4. so

- so는 '그래서, 따라서'라는 뜻으로 절과 절을 연결한다. so 앞의 내용은 원인, 뒤의 내용은 결과를 나타낸다.

  I was sleepy, **so** I went to bed early. 나는 졸려서 일찍 자러 갔다.

  He was very busy, **so** he couldn't have lunch. 그는 매우 바빠서 점심을 먹을 수 없었다.

Check 2 다음 빈칸에 or 또는 so를 쓰시오.

1. Who is younger, Susie _____ Julia?
2. Bill broke my cell phone, _____ I was very angry.
3. Tony will come back Saturday _____ Sunday.

Practice 1　다음 괄호 안에서 알맞은 것을 고르시오.

1. Jenny (and / but) I are good friends.
2. The boy is thin (so / but) strong.
3. The woman is old, (and / but) she looks young.
4. Do you want fish (or / so) meat?
5. I was very sick, (but / so) I was absent from school.
6. Which do you like better, basketball (and / or) baseball?

Practice 2　다음 문장을 주어진 접속사를 이용하여 한 문장으로 연결하시오.

1. I lost my shoes. I was very sad. (so)
   → _____

2. I bought bananas. I bought apples, too. (and)
   → _____

3. He hurt his leg. He couldn't walk. (so)
   → _____

4. Jennifer wants a hat. She wants a skirt, too. (and)
   → _____

5. My brother is young. He is very tall. (but)
   → _____

6. Is your birthday in May? Is your birthday in June? (or)
   → _____

Practice 3　다음 빈칸에 알맞은 접속사를 쓰시오.

1. The boy is handsome _____ smart.
2. Which do you want, chocolate _____ candies?
3. Sally _____ her sister are wearing gloves.
4. I like sports, _____ Emma doesn't like sports.
5. Brad is very kind, _____ I like him.
6. They want to play soccer, _____ they have to do their homework.
7. Tom doesn't drive carefully, _____ his mom is worried about that.
8. Who is taller, Peter _____ David?

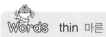 thin 마른　　meat 고기　　absent 결석한　　hurt 다치다　　leg 다리　　carefully 조심스러운

34 | when, before, after

1. when

· 종속접속사는 문장의 중심이 되는 주절과 시간, 이유, 조건 등의 부사적 의미를 가진 종속절을 연결하는 역할을 한다.

· when은 '~할 때'라는 뜻으로 때를 나타내는 절을 이끈다.

He felt tired **when** he came home. 그가 집에 왔을 때 그는 피곤했다.

Susan was cooking **when** I visited her. 내가 그녀를 방문했을 때 Susan은 요리하고 있었다.

＊접속사 when이 이끄는 절에서는 현재시제가 미래시제를 대신한다.

I will take a trip when the vacation starts. 그 방학이 시작할 때 나는 여행을 할 것이다.

Check 1 다음 괄호 안의 단어를 바르게 배열하시오.

1. He didn't answer _____. (I, him, when, called)
2. I learned English _____. (young, I, was, when)
3. Helen was shocked _____. (when, heard, she, that)

---

2. before

· before는 '~하기 전에'라는 뜻으로 시간을 나타내는 절을 이끈다.

Brush your teeth **before** you go to bed. 잠자리에 들기 전에 양치질을 해라.

I turned off the light **before** I went out. 나는 외출하기 전에 그 불을 껐다.

She did her homework **before** she played computer games.

그녀는 컴퓨터 게임을 하기 전에 그녀의 숙제를 했다.

3. after

· after는 '~한 후에'라는 뜻으로 시간을 나타내는 절을 이끈다.

They took a walk **after** they cleaned the house. 그들은 집을 청소한 후에 산책을 했다.

He arrived at the station **after** the train left. 그 기차가 떠난 후에 그는 그 역에 도착했다.

Let's have dinner **after** we finish the work. 우리는 그 일을 끝낸 후에 저녁을 먹자.

＊before와 after는 전치사로도 쓰이는데, 접속사일 때는 뒤에 「주어＋동사」가 오고 전치사일 때는 뒤에 명사가 온다. before lunch, after school

---

Check 2 다음 괄호 안에서 알맞은 것을 고르시오.

1. It gets dark (before / after) the sun sets.
2. Please turn off the computer (before / after) you use it.
3. Close the window (before / after) you go out.

Practice 1 ▍ 다음 괄호 안에서 알맞은 것을 골라 빈칸에 쓰시오.

1. Be careful _____ you drive at night. (after, when)

2. Wash your hands first _____ you have dinner. (before, after)

3. It gets warm _____ you turn on the stove. (before, after)

4. Brush your teeth _____ you go to bed. (before, after)

5. _____ she visited Karl, he was studying English. (When, After)

6. Let's go to the bookstore _____ the class is over. (before, after)

Practice 2 ▍ 다음 우리말과 같도록 빈칸에 알맞은 말을 쓰시오.

1. 나는 일을 끝낸 후에 영화를 볼 것이다.
   = I will watch a movie _____ I finish my work.

2. 그녀가 밖에 나갔을 때 눈이 오기 시작했다.
   = It started snowing _____ she went out.

3. 그 시장에 가기 전에 목록을 작성해라.
   = Make a list _____ you go to the market.

4. 나의 아빠는 피곤할 때 커피를 마신다.
   = My father drinks coffee _____ he feels tired.

5. 그는 쇼핑을 마친 후에 그 극장으로 갔다.
   = He went to the theater _____ he finished shopping.

6. 밖으로 나가기 전에 전등을 꺼라.
   = Turn off the light _____ you go outside.

Practice 3 ▍ 다음 괄호 안의 단어들을 바르게 배열하여 문장을 완성하시오.

1. She learned Japanese _____. (she, young, was, when)

2. He takes a shower _____. (after, exercises, he)

3. They arrived at the station _____. (the train, before, left)

4. He was very tired _____. (he, played, after, badminton)

5. It was still dark _____. (I, this morning, got up, when)

6. We had lunch _____. (we, went, there, before)

7. _____, he writes in a diary. (he, goes to bed, before)

8. _____, Sam visited me. (I, was, when, the library, in)

Words stove 난로   over 끝이 난   outside 밖에   take a shower 샤워하다   still 여전히   diary 일기

35 | that, because, if

1. that

- that은 '~이라는 것, ~한다는 것'이라는 뜻으로 know, think, believe, say, hope 등과 같은 동사의 목적어 역할을 하는 절을 이끈다. that이 목적어 역할을 할 때는 생략할 수 있다.

  I think (**that**) he is a good man. 나는 그가 좋은 남자라고 생각한다.

  She hopes (**that**) he will get better soon. 그녀는 그가 곧 나아지기를 희망한다.

  They believe (**that**) their son is honest. 그들은 그들의 아들이 정직하다고 믿는다.

- *접속사 that이 이끄는 절은 명사 역할을 하며 주어나 보어로도 쓰인다.

  That the man is honest is true. 그 남자가 정직하다는 것은 사실이다. (주어)

  The problem is that he hurt his leg. 그 문제는 그가 그의 다리를 다쳤다는 것이다. (보어)

> **Check 1** 다음 문장에서 **that**이 들어가기에 알맞은 곳을 고르시오.
>
> 1. I ① didn't ② know ③ Sophia ④ likes ⑤ Chris.
> 2. Do ① you ② think ③ the program ④ is ⑤ useful?
> 3. The reporter ① says ② the weather ③ is ④ cold ⑤.

2. because

- because는 '~때문에'라는 뜻으로 원인이나 이유를 나타내는 절을 이끈다.

  I was late for school **because** I got up late. 나는 늦게 일어났기 때문에 학교에 늦었다.

  She closed the window **because** it rained. 비가 왔기 때문에 그녀는 그 창문을 닫았다.

  David is nervous **because** he has a test. David는 시험이 있기 때문에 긴장한다.

3. if

- if는 '만약 ~한다면'이라는 뜻으로 조건을 나타내는 절을 이끈다.

  Exercise regularly **if** you want to be healthy.

  당신이 건강해지기를 원한다면 정기적으로 운동해라.

  You can have this hat **if** you like it. 당신이 이 모자를 좋아하면 그것을 가질 수 있다.

- *접속사 if가 이끄는 절에서는 현재시제가 미래시제를 대신한다.

  I will stay at home if it rains tomorrow. 내일 비가 온다면 나는 집에 머무를 것이다.

> **Check 2** 다음 괄호 안에서 알맞은 것을 고르시오.
>
> 1. I was very sad (because / if) Robert left for Turkey.
> 2. You will see her (because / if) you are on time.
> 3. (Because / If) you feel cold, wear this coat.

Practice 1   다음 괄호 안에서 알맞은 것을 고르시오.

1. He doesn't go to work (because / that) it's Sunday.

2. Ask me (because / if) you have a question.

3. We will go hiking (that / if) it's sunny tomorrow.

4. I don't think (because / that) she is greedy.

5. They believe (if / that) he will become a good man.

6. I can't go to the party (that / because) I hurt my arm.

Practice 2   다음 우리말과 같도록 밑줄 친 부분을 바르게 고치시오.

1. 나는 그가 축구 선수라는 것을 알고 있었다.
   = I knew <u>because</u> he is a soccer player.   → _____

2. 그들은 시간이 없기 때문에 저녁을 먹지 않았다.
   = They didn't have dinner <u>that</u> they had no time.   → _____

3. 네가 바쁘면 나는 그와 함께 갈 것이다.
   = I will go with him <u>because</u> you are busy.   → _____

4. Harry는 종이 한 장을 원한다고 말했다.
   = Harry said <u>if</u> he needed a piece of paper.   → _____

5. 왼쪽으로 돌면 공원을 찾을 수 있을 것이다.
   = <u>Because</u> you turn left, you will find the park.   → _____

Practice 3   다음 문장을 괄호 안의 접속사를 이용하여 한 문장으로 쓰시오.

1. She thinks. He is very smart. (that)
   → _____

2. I can't help you. I have to go now. (because)
   → _____

3. Wear this jacket. You feel cold. (if)
   → _____

4. I know. She is Henry's sister. (that)
   → _____

5. Jay will be happy. You call him. (if)
   → _____

6. I will buy the gloves. They are cheap. (if)
   → _____

 Words greedy 욕심 많은   believe 믿다   turn 돌다   call 전화하다   gloves 장갑   cheap 값이 싼

A. 다음 괄호 안에서 알맞은 것을 고르시오.

1. Julia has a fever (and / but) a runny nose.

2. He is very kind, (because / so) everyone likes him.

3. I believe (that / if) everything will be alright.

4. You should wear your helmet (when / after) you ride a bike.

B. 다음 〈보기〉에서 알맞은 것을 골라 빈칸에 쓰시오.

〈보기〉 or	before	if	but

1. She likes vegetables _____ her brother doesn't like them.

2. He must do his homework _____ he plays soccer.

3. I will meet Susie on Monday _____ on Tuesday.

4. Please tell me _____ you need any help.

C. 다음 우리말과 같도록 알맞은 말을 골라 바르게 배열하시오.

1. 우리는 저녁 식사를 마친 후에 디저트를 먹었다.
   → We ate dessert _____.
   　　　　　　　　(we, dinner, before, after, had)

2. 나는 그가 Betty의 남동생이라는 것을 몰랐다.
   → I didn't know _____.
   　　　　　　　　(he, if, that, is, Betty's brother)

3. 그는 슬플 때 음악을 듣는다.
   → He listens to music _____.
   　　　　　　　　(because, when, sad, he, feels)

D. 다음 두 문장을 괄호 안의 접속사를 이용하여 한 문장으로 쓰시오.

1. She was very angry. Jim told a lie to her. (because)
   → _____

2. You can lose your weight. You exercise regularly. (if)
   → _____

3. He thinks. The novel is great. (that)
   → _____

Words

A. fever 열
   runny nose 콧물이 나오는 코
   helmet 헬멧

B. vegetable 야채
   help 도움

C. dessert 후식, 디저트
   listen to ~을 듣다

D. lie 거짓말
   weight 체중, 무게
   exercise 운동하다
   novel 소설

1. 다음 빈칸에 알맞은 것은?

> It was hot, _____ I turned on the fan.

① but ② or
③ so ④ if
⑤ because

2. 다음 밑줄 친 부분의 쓰임이 어색한 것은?

① The man is handsome <u>and</u> unkind.
② I know <u>that</u> he is a police officer.
③ Knock the door <u>before</u> you enter my room.
④ He enjoys playing soccer <u>and</u> baseball.
⑤ Wash your hands first <u>after</u> you come back.

3. 다음 우리말과 같도록 빈칸에 알맞은 말을 쓰시오.

> 그녀는 운전할 때 선글라스를 쓴다.
> = _____ she drives a car, she wears sunglasses.

→ _____

4. 다음 두 문장을 한 문장으로 바꿀 때 뜻이 같도록 빈칸에 알맞은 말을 쓰시오.

> She is not a singer. She is an actress.
> = She is not a singer _____ an actress.

→ _____

5. 다음 빈칸에 공통으로 알맞은 것은?

> · I will help him _____ he calls me.
> · Please tell me _____ you can't come to the party.

① that ② and
③ before ④ after
⑤ if

6. 다음 빈칸에 들어갈 말이 바르게 짝지어진 것은?

> · I don't like him _____ he is not honest.
> · Did you know _____ she left for Paris?

① because – if ② because – that
③ so – that ④ when – before
⑤ and – because

7. 다음 두 문장을 한 문장으로 연결할 때 빈칸에 알맞은 말을 쓰시오.

> Tina is a cook. Eric is a cook, too.
> → Tina _____ Eric are cooks.

→ _____

8. 다음 문장에서 <u>어색한</u> 부분을 찾아 바르게 고치시오.

> Which do you want, ice cream but a pie for dessert?

_____ → _____

9. 다음 중 when의 쓰임이 나머지와 <u>다른</u> 것은?

① Lucy, when is your birthday?

② Please lock the door when you go out.

③ When she feels tired, she drinks coffee.

④ He was my best friend when I was young.

⑤ When I was in Chicago, I met Lily.

10. 다음 빈칸에 알맞지 <u>않은</u> 것은?

> They _____ that he will like the gift.

① hope   ② think

③ believe   ④ know

⑤ talk

[11-12] 다음 두 문장이 같도록 빈칸에 알맞은 말을 쓰시오.

11.

> My mother is sick, so she is in the hospital.

→ My mother is in the hospital _____ she is sick.

12.

> I brush my teeth before I go to bed.

→ I go to bed _____ I brush my teeth.

[13-14] 다음 빈칸에 알맞은 말을 고르시오.

13.

> It gets bright _____ the sun rises.
>   ~ 후에

① and   ② when

③ but   ④ before

⑤ after

14.

> I lived in the country _____ I was eleven.   ~ 일 때

① and   ② but

③ what   ④ when

⑤ because

15. 다음 밑줄 친 부분이 <u>어색한</u> 것은?

① You can drink juice <u>or</u> coffee.

② Kate bought two apples <u>but</u> an orange.

③ It was a funny movie, <u>so</u> we enjoyed it.

④ The woman is old, <u>but</u> she is healthy.

⑤ I was a chef <u>before</u> I entered the college.

16. 다음 빈칸에 들어갈 말이 나머지와 <u>다른</u> 것은?

① Mike is tall _____ strong.

② The man is poor _____ happy.

③ You _____ she are close friends.

④ I learn art, math, _____ science.

⑤ Tigers are strong _____ fast animals.

Answer Key

Answer Key

Chapter 1. be동사와 대명사

Unit 01. be동사의 현재형과 과거형

Check 1

1. am   2. are   3. is

Check 2

1. was   2. were   3. was

Practice 1

1. They   2. is   3. are   4. She   5. am   6. are   7. are

Practice 2

1. It's a great idea.   2. He's late for the party.
3. They're good singers.   4. We're in the kitchen.
5. I'm a good doctor.   6. You're my best friend.
7. She's fourteen years old.

Practice 3

1. I am a soccer player.   2. It was very big.
3. We were angry at you.   4. They are on the desk.
5. He was at the station.   6. She is smart.
7. You were very tired.

Unit 02. be동사의 부정문과 의문문

Check 1

1. ②   2. ②   3. ②

Check 2

1. Is he an actor?   2. Are you tired?   3. Was she at home?

Practice 1

1. She is not an actress.
2. They were not in the bookstore.
3. He is not absent from school.
4. Alice is not a teacher.
5. Is Julie in the classroom?
6. Are your sneakers new?
7. Was the book interesting?

Practice 2

1. I'm not very tired and sleepy.
2. Was Lisa a famous painter?
3. He was not[wasn't] in his office.
4. Are they good friends?
5. Were my clothes dirty?
6. Is the game very exciting?

7. We are not[aren't] in the bookstore.

Practice 3

1. Yes, I am.   2. No, he isn't.   3. Yes, they were.
4. No, she wasn't.   5. Yes, she is.   6. No, they aren't.
7. Yes, she was.

Unit 03. 인칭대명사와 명사의 소유격

Check 1

1. He   2. We   3. It

Check 2

1. Nick's   2. mother's   3. bird's

Practice 1

1. She   2. It   3. We   4. They   5. They   6. He   7. She

Practice 2

1. my   2. hers   3. your   4. her   5. theirs   6. his   7. mine

Practice 3

1. Leo's   2. Brad's   3. pig's   4. brother's   5. of   6. of
7. of

Unit 04. 지시대명사와 it의 쓰임

Check 1

1. This   2. those   3. these

Check 2

1. 대명사   2. 비인칭 주어   3. 비인칭 주어

Practice 1

1. These   2. That   3. these   4. Those   5. is   6. Are
7. that

Practice 2

1. is big
2. Those buildings are old.
3. That game is exciting.
4. Those dresses are new.
5. That movie is great.
6. This girl is smart.
7. These runners are fast.

Practice 3

1. It, spring   2. It, is   3. Is, sunny   4. It, is   5. It, minutes

128

6. It, is 7. It, dark

Chapter 1: Review Test 1

A. 1. were 2. is 3. Are 4. It's

B. 1. They are not[aren't] my grandparents.
 2. Was James in London two weeks ago?
 3. I'm not a famous musician.
 4. Were you in the same class last year?

C. 1. he 2. Mary's 3. mine, hers 4. they are

D. 1. This is my math teacher.
 2. Those girls are Eric's sisters.
 3. Are these your cats?
 4. It is hot in summer.

Chapter 1: Review Test 2

1. ⑤ 2. ② 3. ⑤ 4. ④ 5. ⑤ 6. ③ 7. ④ 8. ③ 9. ⑤
10. ⑤ 11. ② 12. ③ 13. ① 14. ③ 15. ② 16. ②

1. 두 단어의 관계는 주격과 목적격을 나타낸 것으로 주격 we의 목적격은 us이다.
2. be동사와 not은 줄여서 축약형으로 나타낼 수 있지만, be동사 am과 not은 축약형으로 나타낼 수 없다.
3. 3인칭 단수명사는 be동사 is나 was와 함께 쓴다.
5. was는 be동사 am과 is의 과거형으로 과거를 나타내는 부사(구)와 함께 쓴다.
7. 비인칭 주어 it은 날씨, 날짜, 요일, 계절, 거리, 명암 등의 주어로 사용되며 '그것'이라고 해석하지 않는다.
8. 지시대명사 this와 that은 단수를 나타낼 때 쓰며 be동사 is와 함께 쓰인다. 복수형인 these와 those는 복수를 나타낼 때 쓰며 be동사 are와 함께 쓰인다.
9. 주어에 명사가 올 때 단수명사는 be동사 is와 쓰이고 복수명사는 be동사 are와 함께 쓰인다.
10. her는 she의 목적격과 소유격으로 주격의 자리에는 she가 와야 한다.
16. ours는 we의 소유대명사로 소유격+명사의 의미를 갖고 있으며 ours 뒤에는 명사가 올 수 없다. books의 소유를 나타내므로 we의 소유격인 our가 와야 한다.

Chapter 2. 일반동사

Unit 05. 일반동사의 의미와 형태

Check 1

1. × 2. ○ 3. ○

Check 2

1. fixes 2. walks 3. has 4. reads

Practice 1

1. like 2. starts 3. works 4. lives 5. read 6. plays
7. listen

Practice 2

1. studies 2. does 3. helps 4. teaches 5. comes
6. has 7. watches

Practice 3

1. goes 2. cries 3. buys 4. does 5. finishes 6. cleans
7. wants

Unit 06. 일반동사의 과거형

Check 1

1. watched 2. liked 3. played

Check 2

1. took 2. read 3. ate 4. bought

Practice 1

1. stopped 2. stayed 3. helped 4. had 5. met
6. washed 7. enjoyed

Practice 2

1. took 2. ran 3. sat 4. wrote 5. came 6. ate
7. found

Practice 3

1. played 2. swam 3. put 4. sang 5. read 6. made
7. lost

Unit 07. 일반동사의 부정문과 의문문

Check 1

1. don't 2. doesn't 3. Does

Check 2

1. She did not[didn't] buy a new bag.
2. Did Steve play baseball?

Practice 1

1. He does not[doesn't] have a good friend.
2. Dora did not[didn't] sleep very well.
3. Robert did not[didn't] have an old lamp.
4. My cousin did not[didn't] carry the box.
5. We did not[didn't] listen to music.
6. Judy did not[didn't] make pizza for dinner.

7. She does not[doesn't] teach art at school.

Practice 2
1. Does your sister have 2. Do you like
3. Do they play 4. Did Jessica get
5. Does Charles wash 6. Do they go
7. Did you enjoy

Practice 3
1. I, did 2. he, does 3. No, he 4. she, didn't
5. Yes, he 6. they, do 7. No, he

Chapter 2: Review Test 1
A. 1. have 2. didn't 3. runs 4. Does
B. 1. read 2. bought 3. loved 4. ate 5. went
C. 1. Kevin does not[doesn't] have a nice bike.
   2. Did you find an old coin on the street?
   3. Does your mother cook well?
D. 1. The cat caught a mouse.
   2. Sam and his son sat on the bench.
   3. Did you lose the game?
   4. We did not[didn't] sing then.

Chapter 2: Review Test 2
1. ③ 2. ② 3. ③ 4. ③ 5. ③ 6. Did he buy a new
camera? 7. ② 8. ④ 9. ⑤ 10. ② 11. ③ 12. ③ 13. ③
14. ② 15. ③ 16. ⑤

1. -ch, -sh, -o, -x로 끝나는 동사는 -es를 붙여서 3인칭 단수형을 만든다.
2. 동사에 likes가 온 것으로 보아 주어에는 3인칭 단수형이 와야 한다.
3. last night이라는 과거를 나타내는 부사구가 있는 것으로 보아 과거형 문장이고 동사에 sleep이 있으므로 과거를 나타내는 did가 와야 한다.
4. 과거를 나타내는 부사 ago가 있으므로 go의 과거형이 와야 한다.
5. Janet은 3인칭 단수형이므로 have의 3인칭 단수형인 has가 와야 한다.
7. read의 과거형은 read이며 발음은 달라지므로 주의해야 한다.
9. 일반동사가 있는 문장을 의문문으로 바꿀 때 주어가 1, 2인칭과 3인칭 복수형이면 Do를 사용하고 3인칭 단수형이면 Does를 사용한다. 또한 과거형 문장인 경우에는 Did를 사용한다.
11. 주어가 복수형인 They이므로 do not[don't]을 사용하여 부정문을 만든다.
15. 문장에 과거를 나타내는 부사 yesterday가 있으므로 동사에 현재형이 올 수 없다.

Chapter 3. 명사와 관사
Unit 08. 명사의 단수와 복수
Check 1
1. ○ 2. × 3. × 4. ×

Check 2
1. children 2. leaves 3. cities 4. feet

Practice 1
1. umbrellas 2. buses 3. knives 4. potatoes 5. hats
6. roofs 7. men 8. sheep 9. babies 10. women
11. dishes 12. oxen 13. toys 14. teachers

Practice 2
1. teeth 2. photos 3. fish 4. tomatoes 5. countries
6. houses 7. ladies

Practice 3
1. books 2. gloves 3. water 4. pairs 5. pianos
6. pieces 7. puppies

Unit 09. 부정관사와 정관사
Check 1
1. an 2. a 3. an

Check 2
1. × 2. ○ 3. ○

Practice 1
1. an 2. The 3. a 4. a 5. the 6. the 7. an

Practice 2
1. × 2. × 3. the 4. × 5. × 6. the 7. the

Practice 3
1. a new cell phone 2. a nice garden 3. by bus
4. two hours a day 5. in the sky 6. a blue hat

Chapter 3: Review Test 1
A. 1. cities 2. boxes 3. × 4. men 5. × 6. wolves
   7. deer 8. boys 9. × 10. feet
B. 1. an 2. a 3. the 4. The, the 5. ×
C. 1. Happiness 2. buses 3. pieces of cheese
   4. leaves
D. 1. after school 2. a glass of milk 3. have dinner
   4. the west

Chapter 3: Review Test 2

1. ② 2. ② 3. ④ 4. ④ 5. ③ 6. ④ 7. ⑤ 8. ③ 9. ③
10. ② 11. ② 12. ⑤ 13. ⑤ 14. ① 15. ⑤ 16. ②

1. photo의 복수형은 photos로 -s만 붙인다.
2. -f(e)로 끝나는 단어는 보통 f(e)를 v로 바꾸고 -es를 붙이지만 roof는 예외적인 단어로 -s를 붙여서 복수형을 만든다.
3. 명사 앞에 형용사가 있는 경우에는 형용사의 첫소리 글자에 따라서 a나 an을 붙인다.
4. sheep은 단수형과 복수형이 같은 명사이다.
5. '일주일에 한 번'이라고 할 때는 부정관사 a를 사용하여 once a week 라고 한다.
6. 셀 수 없는 명사는 복수형으로 만들 수 없다.
9. -ch로 끝나는 명사는 -es를 붙여서 복수형을 만든다.
10. 셀 수 없는 명사 앞에는 부정관사 a나 an을 붙이지 않는다.
12. 식사나 과목명 앞에는 관사를 붙이지 않는다.
15. 명사가 본래의 목적으로 사용될 때는 관사를 붙이지 않는다.
16. 악기 앞에는 정관사 the를 붙인다.

Chapter 4. 동사의 시제

Unit 10. 현재시제와 과거시제

Check 1

1. play 2. is 3. has

Check 2

1. was 2. went 3. rode

Practice 1

1. read 2. get 3. watched 4. goes 5. heard 6. planted
7. drinks

Practice 2

1. has 2. lost 3. brushes 4. fall 5. listened 6. stayed
7. goes

Practice 3

1. has 2. had 3. is 4. was 5. go 6. sang 7. baked

Unit 11. 진행시제의 쓰임과 형태

Check 1

1. cutting 2. cleaning 3. dying 4. baking

Check 2

1. drawing 2. building

Practice 1

1. is washing 2. is drinking 3. am doing 4. is reading
5. are cooking 6. are waiting 7. is playing

Practice 2

1. He was writing a letter to his friend.
2. The wind is blowing hard today.
3. I am drawing a picture in the park.
4. The boy was running fast to the store.
5. My dad is having dinner at home.
6. She was making a cake for Peter.
7. They are selling hats and bags there.

Practice 3

1. He is not[isn't] inventing something.
2. Were eagles flying away?
3. Ted was washing the car.
4. Kids were not[weren't] playing soccer.
5. A dog was not[wasn't] barking then.
6. Babies were sleeping on the bed.
7. Carol is collecting foreign coins.

Unit 12. 미래시제(will, be going to)

Check 1

1. be 2. will not 3. visit

Check 2

1. going to 2. Are 3. is not going

Practice 1

1. going to see 2. won't stay 3. will arrive
4. are going to 5. will pass 6. is not going
7. to have

Practice 2

1. He is not going to play tennis.
2. This autumn will be very cool.
3. She will buy new sneakers.
4. Will my father drive a truck?
5. She is going to take a rest.
6. I am not going to drink coffee.
7. They won't be busy tomorrow.

Practice 3

1. Will 2. Is, Yes 3. going, it, is 4. Will, Yes, he
5. No, they 6. I'm, not 7. No, she

Chapter 4: Review Test 1

A. 1. invited 2. reads 3. is 4. visited

B. 1. snowed 2. Is 3. was 4. travel

C. 1. will, call 2. was, not 3. are, sitting 4. Is, waiting

D. 1. The baby was crying on the bed.

   2. I'm not going to write a letter tonight.

   3. Are they going to learn Chinese?

   4. He will go hiking with his family.

Chapter 4: Review Test 2

1. ⑤ 2. ④ 3. ② 4. ③ 5. ① 6. ③ 7. ② 8. ③ 9. ④
10. ① 11. ② 12. ① 13. ⑤ 14. ② 15. ④ 16. ⑤

1. 동사의 -ing형을 만들 때, 대부분의 동사는 뒤에 -ing를 붙이고 -e로 끝나는 동사는 e를 삭제하고 -ing를 붙이며 -ie로 끝나는 동사는 ie를 y로 바꾸고 -ing를 붙인다.

2. 과거의 사실을 나타낼 때, 동사는 과거형으로 나타낸다.

3. 진행형은 「be동사+동사의 -ing형」으로 나타내며 makes가 있는 것으로 보아 현재형이고 주어가 My brother로 3인칭 단수형이므로 be동사 is를 사용하여 만든다.

4. 현재를 나타내는 부사 now는 미래를 나타내는 조동사 will과 함께 쓸 수 없다.

5. 미래를 나타내는 조동사 will은 be going to로 바꿀 수 있으며 주어가 I이므로 be동사 am을 쓴다.

6. 현재의 사실이나 진리는 항상 현재형으로 나타낸다.

8. every morning은 매일 반복적인 동작을 나타내는 부사구로 현재형 동사가 와야 하고 last night은 과거를 나타내는 부사구로 과거형 동사가 와야 한다.

9. 피곤해서 오후에 바이올린 연습을 하지 않을 것이라는 뜻이 되도록 will not(won't)을 사용하는 미래시제 부정문이 와야 한다.

10. be going to 뒤에 명사가 오면 진행형 문장이고 뒤에 동사가 오면 미래를 나타낸다.

12. 주어가 3인칭 단수라도 조동사 will 뒤에 -s를 붙이지 않으며 will 뒤에는 항상 동사원형이 온다.

13. tomorrow는 미래를 나타내는 부사이다.

15. 진행형 문장을 만들 때 주어가 3인칭 단수일 경우에는 be동사 is를 쓰고 과거를 나타낼 때는 was를 쓴다.

Chapter 5. 의문사

Unit 13. who, whose, what, which

Check 1

1. Whose 2. Who 3. Who

Check 2

1. What 2. Which 3. What

Practice 1

1. Which 2. Who 3. Whose/What 4. Which 5. What
6. What 7. What

Practice 2

1. Whose 2. Who 3. What 4. Which 5. Whose
6. Which 7. Who

Practice 3

1. What did James make?

2. Whose red cap is that?

3. Who met Lucy yesterday?

4. Who is your favorite actor?

5. Whose is this big boat?

6. What did you eat for lunch?

7. Which season do you like, spring or fall?

Unit 14. when, where, why

Check 1

1. When 2. When 3. Where

Check 2

1. Because 2. Why

Practice 1

1. When 2. When 3. Where 4. Why 5. Where 6. When
7. Why

Practice 2

1. Where 2. When 3. Why 4. When 5. Why 6. Where
7. When

Practice 3

1. Where did they play basketball?

2. Why do you like this scarf?

3. Where is the bakery?

4. When did John hurt his finger?

5. Where were you last Friday?

6. When does the bookstore close?

7. Why do you like the actress?

Unit 15. how, how+형용사/부사

Check 1

1. How, is 2. How, does, he

Check 2

1. How much 2. How long 3. How often

Practice 1

1. long 2. much 3. far 4. old 5. tall 6. many 7. often

Practice 2

1. much 2. far 3. many 4. How 5. How 6. often
7. long

Practice 3

1. How 2. How long 3. How many 4. How old
5. How often 6. How long 7. How tall

Chapter 5: Review Test 1

A. 1. Whose 2. How 3. Which 4. When
B. 1. Who, is 2. Why, did 3. Where, did
C. 1. How often do you clean your room?
   2. How tall is she?
   3. When do you get up every day?
D. 1. Where, did 2. Who, wrote 3. What/Which, bus
   4. Why, were

Chapter 5: Review Test 2

1. ② 2. ⑤ 3. ② 4. ⑤ 5. ⑤ 6. Who 7. ① 8. ④
9. ⑤ 10. ④ 11. ① 12. ④ 13. ① 14. ② 15. ③ 16. ③

2. 사물이나 물건 등을 물어볼 때는 의문사 What을 쓴다.

3. 셀 수 있는 명사를 '얼마나 많이 ~?'라고 표현할 때는 How many ~? 를 쓴다.

4. 방법이나 정도를 나타낼 때는 의문사 How를 쓴다.

5. 누구의 것인지를 물어보면 소유대명사나 「소유격+명사」의 형태로 답한 다.

6. 사람을 물어볼 때는 의문사 Who를 쓴다.

7. How long ~?은 사물의 길이나 시간을 나타낼 때 사용하며 여기서는 영화의 시간을 물어보고 있다.

8. 늦은 이유와 언제 일어났는지를 물어보고 있으므로 이유를 물어보는 Why와 시간을 물어보는 When이 와야 한다.

9. 키를 물어볼 때는 How tall ~?을 쓴다.

13. When을 사용하여 시간을 물어보고 있으므로 시간에 해당하는 답이 와야 한다.

14. How many 뒤에는 셀 수 있는 명사의 복수형이 오고 How much 뒤 에는 셀 수 없는 명사가 온다.

16. bread는 셀 수 없는 명사이므로 How much로 물어봐야 한다.

Chapter 6. 조동사

Unit 16. can, will, may

Check 1

1. read 2. will 3. cannot

Check 2

1. may 2. May

Practice 1

1. drive 2. clean 3. be 4. read 5. drink 6. goes
7. swims

Practice 2

1. She can make 2. Can you help
3. The test may not be 4. He may go to Japan
5. They may get 6. May I use
7. Can the baby turn

Practice 3

1. I will plant trees in the garden.
2. They will go to Paris by airplane.
3. She may be late for the meeting.
4. Bill will study hard for the exam.
5. My friend and I can go shopping.
6. I can wait for Ann at the bus stop.
7. He may read books in the library.

Unit 17. must, have to, should

Check 1

1. play 2. has 3. Does

Check 2

1. early 2. should

Practice 1

1. do 2. buy 3. help 4. take 5. get 6. hurry 7. tell

Practice 2

1. I have to walk 2. We must keep
3. must study late 4. must be hungry
5. The woman has to do 6. must be honest
7. must be a lawyer

Practice 3

1. should not 2. exercise 3. has to 4. eat 5. take
6. be 7. cross

Chapter 6: Review Test 1

A. 1. can't 2. may 3. doesn't have to 4. must

B. 1. Does Nick have to wait for the truck?

2. You should not[shouldn't] leave here now.

3. Will it be sunny this afternoon?

4. I have to work next Sunday.

C. 1. must not 2. have to 3. doesn't 4. listen

D. ②

Chapter 6: Review Test 2

1. ① 2. ③ 3. ④ 4. ⑤ 5. ⑤ 6. ③ 7. ⑤ 8. ④ 9. ④
10. may 11. ② 12. ③ 13. ③ 14. ⑤ 15. ② 16. ②

1. 동사 play가 있으므로 동사 앞에 올 수 있는 것은 조동사이다.

2. next year라는 미래를 나타내는 부사구가 있으므로 미래형 문장을 만들기 위해 조동사 will이 있어야 한다.

3. 조동사 may는 약한 추측이나 허가를 나타낼 때 사용한다.

4. 조동사 must는 강한 추측이나 의무를 나타낼 때 사용한다.

5. 의무를 나타내는 must는 have to로 바꾸어 쓸 수 있으며 주어가 3인칭 단수형이므로 has to가 와야 한다.

7. 조동사의 의문문에 대한 대답은 Yes나 No를 사용하여 조동사로 답한다.

8. 조동사는 한 문장에 2개를 동시에 사용할 수 없으므로 can을 be able to로 바꾸고 be 앞에서 will을 넣어서 나타낸다.

9. 조동사 can 뒤에는 항상 동사원형이 온다.

11. 조동사 뒤에는 동사원형이 오며 부정문은 조동사 뒤에 not을 붙여 만든다.

14. must는 '~해야 한다'라는 의무와 '~임에 틀림없다'라는 강한 추측을 나타내는데 문장에서 의미를 잘 파악해야 한다.

Chapter 7. 형용사와 부사

Unit 18. 형용사

Check 1

1. big 2. famous 3. kind

Check 2

1. many 2. much 3. some

Practice 1

1. handsome man

2. exciting movie

3. They are popular singers.

4. She is a beautiful woman.

5. It is a fresh peach.

6. It is an expensive car.

7. They are cheap gloves.

Practice 2

1. any 2. Many 3. any 4. some 5. many 6. much
7. any

Practice 3

1. Look at that small monkey!

2. I bought a black cap.

3. He has a nice garden.

4. The cat is small and cute.

5. The girl has big eyes.

6. The woman wants new shoes.

Unit 19. 부사

Check 1

1. badly 2. easily 3. late 4. well 5. long 6. simply

Check 2

1. sometimes 2. often 3. never

Practice 1

1. happily 2. slowly 3. dangerous 4. good 5. late
6. quickly 7. well

Practice 2

1. ① 2. ① 3. ② 4. ① 5. ② 6. ② 7. ①

Practice 3

1. slowly 2. high 3. really hot 4. easily 5. often goes
6. well 7. heavily

Unit 20. 비교급과 최상급

Check 1

1. prettier, prettiest 2. more exciting, most exciting

Check 2

1. older 2. heaviest 3. popular

Practice 1

1. richer, richest 2. bigger, biggest 3. better, best

4. larger, largest 5. more, most

6. more useful, most useful 7. worse, worst

Practice 2

1. biggest 2. brighter 3. heavier 4. colder 5. cutest

6. best　7. bravest

Practice 3

1. longest　2. smartest　3. young　4. most　5. strong

6. most　7. colder

Chapter 7: Review Test 1

A. 1. any　2. a lot of　3. much　4. some

B. 1. Nick often exercises in the gym.

　2. She can never find her hairpin.

　3. It is usually rainy and hot in summer.

　4. My sister always goes to the library on Sunday.

C. 1. late　2. easily　3. quietly　4. good

D. 1. comfortable as

　2. not as[so] cold

　3. the largest island

　4. more popular than

Chapter 7: Review Test 2

1. ③　2. ②　3. ③　4. ②　5. ⑤　6. ④　7. ④　8. ⑤

9. It is really cold today.　10. ④　11. ④

12. more expensive　13. ①　14. ④　15. ①　16. ②

1. 형용사와 부사의 관계로 구성되어 있는데 much와 more는 원급과 비교급을 나타낸다. much는 형용사와 부사의 형태가 같다.

2. 비교급과 최상급으로 만들 때 -y로 끝나는 단어는 y를 i로 바꾸고 -er과 -est를 붙인다.

3. high, safe, easy, happy는 모두 형용사이고 school은 명사이다.

4. fast는 형용사와 부사의 형태가 같은 단어로 명사 앞에 쓰인 fast는 형용사이다.

5. a lot of는 '많은'이라는 뜻으로 셀 수 있는 명사와 셀 수 없는 명사 앞에 모두 사용할 수 있다. 셀 수 있는 명사 앞에 있는 a lot of는 many로 바꿔 쓸 수 있다.

6. some은 긍정문에 사용하고 any는 부정문과 의문문에 사용하는데, 권유를 나타낼 때는 some을 사용한다.

7. 셀 수 없는 명사 앞에는 many가 아닌 much를 사용한다.

8. 빈도부사는 빈도를 나타내는 부사로 일반동사 앞에, be동사나 조동사 뒤에 위치한다.

10. 「비교급+than」은 '~보다 더 ~한'이라는 뜻으로 비교급 문장에 쓰인다.

11. -ful, -ous 등의 형용사나 3음절 이상의 형용사는 앞에 more를 붙여서 비교급을 만든다.

16. 빈도부사는 일반동사 앞에 위치하므로 usually have의 형태가 되어야 한다.

Chapter 8. 문장의 종류

Unit 21. 명령문과 청유문

Check 1

1. Wash　2. Don't be　3. Sit

Check 2

1. 산책하자.　2. 그 음식을 먹지 말자.

3. 이번 주말에 낚시하러 가자.

Practice 1

1. Open the window.　2. Do your homework.

3. Be kind to everyone.　4. Put on your jacket.

5. Drive the car slowly.　6. Be quiet in the library.

7. Make a birthday card.

Practice 2

1. Don't leave　2. Don't be　3. Don't build　4. Don't waste

5. Don't talk　6. Don't take　7. Don't drink

Practice 3

1. go　2. meet　3. play　4. eat　5. make　6. Let's not

7. Let's

Unit 22. 감탄문

Check 1

1. What a pretty　2. wonderful pants　3. they are

Check 2

1. How　2. What　3. How

Practice 1

1. How　2. What　3. How　4. What　5. What　6. How

7. What

Practice 2

1. What an old　2. How high　3. How heavy　4. How early

5. How beautiful　6. What a busy　7. What amazing

Practice 3

1. How → What　2. What → How　3. are they → they are

4. a → an　5. How → What　6. What → How　7. ? → !

Unit 23. 부가의문문과 선택의문문

Check 1

1. aren't you　2. did she　3. won't they

Check 2

1. or, cold 2. Which, or

Practice 1

1. is 2. wasn't 3. won't 4. were 5. did 6. didn't
7. can't

Practice 2

1. will she 2. didn't you 3. doesn't she 4. aren't you
5. can't she 6. were you 7. did they

Practice 3

1. or 2. or 3. Which, or 4. Who, or 5. or, hers
6. Is, or

Chapter 8: Review Test 1

A. 1. What, a, sad 2. How, nice 3. What, colorful
   4. How, difficult
B. 1. Let's, Yes 2. or, like 3. isn't, Yes, is
C. 1. Don't take pictures here.
   2. Sean moved here last month, didn't he?
   3. What expensive furniture it is!
   4. How heavy the box is!
D. 1. How, sweet 2. or, baseball 3. will, he

Chapter 8: Review Test 2

1. ④ 2. ② 3. ② 4. ① 5. ③ 6. ③ 7. drives, drive
8. What, a, big, How, big 9. ④ 10. aren't they 11. ②
12. ④ 13. ⑤ 14. ④ 15. ② 16. ②

1. 부정명령문은 「Don't+동사원형」의 형태이다.
2. 제안문의 부정문은 Let's 뒤에 not을 넣어서 나타낸다.
3. 감탄문은 What이나 How를 사용하여 나타내는데 How 뒤에는 형용사
가 오고 What 뒤에는 「형용사+명사」가 온다.
5. 조동사가 있는 문장의 부가의문문은 문장에 있는 조동사를 이용하여 만
들며 앞이 긍정이면 뒤에 부정이 온다.
6. or를 사용한 선택의문문의 대답은 둘 중에 하나를 선택해서 답한다.
10. 문장에 be동사 are가 있으므로 부가의문문은 부정인 aren't를 쓴다.
14. 문장에 조동사 can't가 있으므로 부가의문문은 긍정인 can을 쓴다.

Chapter 9. to부정사와 동명사

Unit 24. to부정사 1

Check 1

1. to read 2. To make 3. to play

Check 2

1. 피아노를 연주하는 것은
2. 그 남자를 만나기를
3. 책들을 읽는 것이다

Practice 1

1. 보어 2. 목적어 3. 목적어 4. 주어 5. 보어 6. 목적어
7. 보어

Practice 2

1. swim 2. to get 3. to travel 4. meet 5. go 6. sing
7. keep

Practice 3

1. like to eat 2. decided to go on a picnic 3. is to ride
4. To get up early 5. began to make 6. want to have

Unit 25. to부정사 2

Check 1

1. something 2. a dress 3. comic books

Check 2

1. 그 시험에 합격해서 2. 요리사가 되었다 3. Jim을 만나기 위해

Practice 1

1. to drink 2. to sit 3. to think 4. to buy 5. to read
6. to write 7. to eat[have]

Practice 2

1. 그 소식을 들어서 2. 운동하기 위해 3. 미술을 공부하기 위해
4. 95세까지 5. 작가가 되었다 6. 바나나들을 사기 위해
7. 당신을 다시 만나서

Practice 3

1. She found a place to hide in.
2. We were so surprised to see him.
3. Tom went to a bookstore to buy books.
4. There was no water to drink.

Unit 26. 동명사

Check 1

1. 주어 2. 보어 3. 목적어

Check 2

1. watching 2. drinking 3. to read

Practice 1

1. playing　2. coming　3. to take　4. to see　5. taking
6. to eat　7. listening

Practice 2

1. doing　2. to watch　3. answering　4. to travel　5. to use
6. finding　7. working

Practice 3

1. getting　2. laughing　3. eat　4. watching　5. draw
6. read　7. ride

Chapter 9: Review Test 1

A. 1. to meet　2. cooking　3. going skiing　4. to build
B. 1. ⓒ　2. ⓓ　3. ⓑ　4. ⓐ
C. 1. to see　2. get　3. changing　4. to take
D. 1. to lose my wallet　2. to say goodbye
　　3. to stay here　4. reading magazines

Chapter 9: Review Test 2

1. ②　2. ④　3. ③　4. ⑤　5. ②　6. My dog enjoys taking a
bath.　7. ③　8. ②　9. ④　10. ②　11. ③　12. ①　13. ①
14. ③　15. ⑤　16. ④

1. decide 뒤에는 목적어로 to부정사가 온다.
3. hope 뒤에는 to부정사가 오며 전치사 뒤에는 명사나 대명사가 올 수
있는데 동사가 올 경우에는 동명사가 온다.
4. like 뒤에는 목적어로 to부정사, 동명사 둘다 올 수 있다.
7. to 뒤에 동사가 오면 to부정사로 쓰이고 to 뒤에 명사가 오면 전치사로
쓰인다.
8. finish 뒤에 동사가 올 경우에는 동명사가 온다.
9. learn은 목적어로 to부정사가 온다.
10. 「grow up+to부정사」는 '자라서 ~이 되다'라는 뜻의 부사적 용법으
로 결과를 나타낸다.
12. to부정사가 주어로 사용되는 경우 가주어 it을 사용하여 to부정사를 뒤
로 이동할 수 있다.
14. want 뒤에는 목적어로 to부정사가 온다.

Chapter 10. 문장의 형태
Unit 27. There is/are, 감각동사
Check 1

1. is　2. are　3. Is

Check 2

1. soft　2. angry　3. sweet

Practice 1

1. are　2. is　3. aren't　4. is　5. isn't　6. aren't　7. are

Practice 2

1. Is there　2. Are there　3. Are there, there are
4. Is there, there isn't　5. Is there, there isn't
6. Is there, there is　7. Are there, there are

Practice 3

1. looks　2. smells　3. sounds　4. looks　5. feels　6. taste
7. felt

Unit 28. 4형식 문장과 수여동사
Check 1

1. me　2. gave　3. pizza

Check 2

1. to　2. for　3. of

Practice 1

1. He asked me questions.　2. She made us pizza.
3. Emily told him a story.　4. He gave them pencils.
5. I will show you my room.　6. Ann bought us erasers.
7. Jim wrote her a letter.

Practice 2

1. of　2. to　3. to　4. for　5. for　6. to　7. to

Practice 3

1. David gave a birthday present to him.
2. We made a big chocolate cake for Lisa.
3. Daniel bought a yellow scarf for his mom.
4. My sister asked a strange question of me.
5. Mr. Johnson taught history to them.
6. My aunt cooked spaghetti for her daughter.

Unit 29. 5형식 문장과 목적격보어
Check 1

1. cool　2. upset　3. Joe

Check 2

1. to help　2. to clean　3. to come

Practice 1

1. him　2. happy　3. warm　4. boring　5. baby　6. made
7. healthy

Practice 2
1. to help 2. to call 3. to use 4. to go 5. to study
6. to join 7. to drive

Practice 3
1. you safe 2. the box empty 3. her son to go out
4. her to get up early 5. me to visit her house
6. him to eat vegetables 7. my friend to take pictures

Chapter 10: Review Test 1
A. 1. 간접목적어 2. 주격보어 3. 직접목적어 4. 목적격보어
B. 1. to go 2. for 3. good 4. Is
C. 1. tastes, terrible 2. There, are, many, kites
   3. made, pizza, for, me
D. 1. study → to study 2. aren't → isn't
   3. tiredly → tired 4. for → to

Chapter 10: Review Test 2
1. ⑤ 2. ④ 3. to 4. ② 5. ① 6. ② 7. ② 8. ① 9. ④
10. ① 11. ⑤ 12. take → to take 13. ① 14. ③ 15. ⑤
16. ②

1. 셀 수 없는 명사는 단수 취급하며 There is를 사용하여 나타낸다.
2. feel, smell, sound, look, taste 등의 감각동사 뒤에는 형용사가 온다.
3. 4형식 문장을 3형식 문장으로 전환할 때 teach, show 등의 동사는 간접목적어 앞에 전치사 to를 사용한다.
4. 4형식 문장을 3형식 문장으로 전환할 때 ask는 간접목적어 앞에 전치사 of를, make는 for를 사용한다.
7. 4형식 문장을 3형식 문장으로 전환할 때 buy, cook, make 등의 동사는 간접목적어 앞에 전치사 for를 사용한다.
12. 5형식 문장의 목적격보어에는 to부정사가 올 수도 있는데, 이 경우에는 목적어의 행동을 설명해 준다.
16. want는 목적격보어에 to부정사를 쓴다.

Chapter 11. 전치사
Unit 30. 시간의 전치사
Check 1
1. at 2. in 3. on

Check 2
1. 2시간 동안 2. 10시 전에 3. 여름 축제 동안

Practice 1
1. in 2. at 3. on 4. at 5. on 6. on

Practice 2
1. for 2. before 3. during 4. for 5. before 6. during

Practice 3
1. before 2. on 3. for 4. in 5. at 6. in 7. during

Unit 31. 장소와 위치의 전치사
Check 1
1. in 2. in 3. at

Check 2
1. under 2. across from 3. near

Practice 1
1. at 2. at 3. in 4. in 5. at 6. in

Practice 2
1. on 2. behind 3. near 4. by 5. across from
6. in front of

Practice 3
1. near 2. next to[by] 3. behind 4. across from
5. under 6. on 7. between, and

Unit 32. 다양한 쓰임의 전치사
Check 1
1. 그 나무 위로 2. 그 숲 안으로 3. 뉴욕을 향하여

Check 2
1. by 2. with 3. around

Practice 1
1. about 2. with 3. by 4. up 5. without 6. down

Practice 2
1. for 2. into 3. up 4. from 5. around 6. for

Practice 3
1. around 2. into 3. without 4. with 5. to 6. out of
7. for

Chapter 11: Review Test 1
A. 1. in, in 2. on, on 3. At, at
B. 1. for 2. from 3. from 4. before
C. 1. under 2. between 3. after 4. near
D. 1. from Monday to Friday

2. walked without an umbrella

3. take a trip during the summer vacation

4. rolled down the hill

Chapter 11: Review Test 2

1. ⑤ 2. ② 3. ② 4. by 5. to → of 6. ① 7. ③ 8. about
9. ⑤ 10. ② 11. for 12. during 13. ④ 14. ① 15. ③
16. ②

1. 요일 앞에는 전치사 on을 쓴다.

2. 특정한 날을 나타낼 때는 전치사 on을 쓴다.

3. 계절 앞에는 전치사 in을 사용하고 시각 앞에는 전치사 at을 사용한다.

5. '~ 앞에'를 나타낼 때는 in front of를 쓴다.

9. '~ 동안'이라는 구체적인 시간을 나타낼 때는 전치사 for를 쓴다.

10. during 뒤에는 특정 시기가 오고 for 뒤에는 주로 일정한 기간을 나타내는 숫자가 온다.

13. 교통수단을 나타낼 때는 전치사 by를 사용하여 「by+교통수단」으로 나타낸다.

16. 전치사 in은 연도나 계절, 월 앞에 사용하여 시간을 나타낸다.

Chapter 12. 접속사

Unit 33. and, but, or, so

Check 1

1. and 2. and 3. but

Check 2

1. or 2. so 3. or

Practice 1

1. and 2. but 3. but 4. or 5. so 6. or

Practice 2

1. I lost my shoes so I was very sad.

2. I bought bananas and apples.

3. He hurt his leg so he couldn't walk.

4. Jennifer wants a hat and a skirt.

5. My brother is young but (he is) very tall.

6. Is your birthday in May or in June?

Practice 3

1. and 2. or 3. and 4. but 5. so 6. but 7. so 8. or

Unit 34. when, before, after

Check 1

1. when I called him 2. when I was young

3. when she heard that

Check 2

1. after 2. after 3. before

Practice 1

1. when 2. before 3. after 4. before 5. When 6. after

Practice 2

1. after 2. when 3. before 4. when 5. after 6. before

Practice 3

1. when she was young 2. after he exercises

3. before the train left 4. after he played badminton

5. when I got up this morning 6. before we went there

7. Before he goes to bed 8. When I was in the library

Unit 35. that, because, if

Check 1

1. ③ 2. ③ 3. ②

Check 2

1. because 2. if 3. If

Practice 1

1. because 2. if 3. if 4. that 5. that 6. because

Practice 2

1. that 2. because 3. if 4. that 5. If

Practice 3

1. She thinks that he is very smart.

2. I can't help you because I have to go now.

3. Wear this jacket if you feel cold.

4. I know that she is Henry's sister.

5. Jay will be happy if you call him.

6. I will buy the gloves if they are cheap.

Chapter 12: Review Test 1

A. 1. and 2. so 3. that 4. when

B. 1. but 2. before 3. or 4. if

C. 1. after we had dinner

   2. that he is Betty's brother

   3. when he feels sad

D. 1. She was very angry because Jim told a lie to her.

   2. You can lose your weight if you exercise regularly.

3. He thinks that the novel is great.

Chapter 12: Review Test 2

1. ③ 2. ① 3. When 4. but 5. ⑤ 6. ② 7. and
8. but → or 9. ① 10. ⑤ 11. because 12. after 13. ⑤
14. ④ 15. ② 16. ②

1. 더워서 선풍기를 켰다는 뜻으로 원인과 결과를 나타내기 때문에 접속사 so를 쓴다.

2. 잘생겼지만 불친절하다고 했으므로 접속사 but을 쓴다.

5. 조건을 나타낼 때는 접속사 if를 쓴다.

6. 접속사 that은 '~이라는 것, ~한다는 것'이라는 뜻으로 know, think, believe, say, hope 등과 같은 동사의 목적어 역할을 하는 절을 이끈다.

8. 둘 중에 선택을 나타내는 경우에는 접속사 or를 쓴다.

9. when이 의문사로 쓰이면 '언제'라는 뜻이고 접속사로 쓰이면 '~할 때'라는 뜻이다.

16. 접속사 and는 '~와, 그리고'라는 뜻으로 서로 비슷한 내용을 연결하며 접속사 but은 '그러나, 하지만'의 뜻으로 서로 반대되는 내용을 연결한다.

Workbook

와우내

Let's Study!

The
Grammar
School

새로운 중학교 교과 과정 반영

내신 대비 문제와 주관식 문제 수록

다양한 문제 풀이를 통한 응용령 향상

예비
중학

Iambooks

Let's Study!

The Grammar School 예비중학

Workbook

I am books

Exercise 1 다음 문장을 축약형을 사용해 부정문으로 고치시오.

1. He is an artist.
   → _____

2. They are farmers.
   → _____

3. It is our house.
   → _____

4. She is his sister.
   → _____

5. Her daughter is very tall.
   → _____

6. My father is in the hospital.
   → _____

7. We are twelve years old.
   → _____

8. He is tired and sleepy.
   → _____

Exercise 2 다음 문장을 의문문으로 고치시오.

1. You are busy.
   → _____

2. She is from Canada.
   → _____

3. The children are in the park.
   → _____

4. You are a good singer.
   → _____

5. They are interesting.
   → _____

6. The stores are open today.
   → _____

7. John and Ann are cooks.
   → _____

다음 문장의 괄호 안에서 알맞은 인칭대명사를 고르시오.

1. Put on (you, your) coat.

2. (They, Their, Them) like grapes.

3. (I, My, Me) teacher is very kind.

4. I have a puppy. I love (its, it, them).

5. (We, Our, Us) catch five big fish.

6. She gives me (she, her) pencil.

7. I have a son. I like (he, him, his).

8. Do you know (they, them)?

9. (They, Them, Their) are late for the meeting.

10. She teaches (I, me, my) music.

다음 문장에서 밑줄 친 부분을 바르게 고치시오.

1. These woman is beautiful.　→ _____

2. He likes this gloves.　→ _____

3. That is his robots.　→ _____

4. That watch are very cheap.　→ _____

5. These are your bag.　→ _____

6. Those book are very thick.　→ _____

7. This rings is expensive.　→ _____

8. These room are dirty.　→ _____

9. This is snowing today.　→ _____

10. These flower are for you.　→ _____

Exercise 1 | 다음 문장의 괄호 안에서 알맞은 동사를 고르시오.

1. The baby (cry, cries) in the room.

2. I (play, plays) the piano after school.

3. He (wash, washes) his car.

4. She (have, has) two daughters.

5. It (rain, rains) a lot in summer.

6. Peter (want, wants) the red hat.

7. She and I (come, comes) home late.

8. Many people (walk, walks) on the street.

9. The leaves (fall, falls) on the ground.

10. Jane (do, does) her homework at night.

Exercise 2 | 다음 주어진 동사를 이용해 과거 문장을 완성하시오.

1. I _____ Carol at the corner. (see)

2. She _____ cake a few minutes ago. (eat)

3. He _____ three cats before. (have)

4. They _____ really hungry then. (be)

5. Julia _____ David last week. (meet)

6. Mom _____ me a camera last Sunday. (buy)

7. We _____ a big house two months ago. (build)

8. I _____ camping with my family. (go)

9. There _____ a doll on the table. (be)

10. Mom _____ us cookies last weekend. (make)

다음 문장의 괄호 안에서 알맞은 것을 고르시오.

1. I (don't like, don't likes) carrots.

2. He (doesn't drink, doesn't drinks) juice.

3. We (don't want, doesn't want) the pizza.

4. She (don't have, doesn't have) dinner.

5. James (don't teach, doesn't teach) science.

6. (Do you speak, Do you speaks) Korean?

7. (Does Amy study, Does Amy studies) English?

8. (Do you choose, Do you chooses) him a present?

9. (Do they carries, Do they carry) their bags?

10. (Does Jim and you leave, Do Jim and you leave) at nine?

다음 문장을 지시대로 바꿔 쓰시오.

1. He read a newspaper yesterday. (부정문으로)
   → _____

2. My father was a firefighter. (부정문으로)
   → _____

3. We went to the market. (부정문으로)
   → _____

4. Brian did his homework. (부정문으로)
   → _____

5. You were late for school then. (의문문으로)
   → _____

6. Ann visited her uncle. (의문문으로)
   → _____

7. He sent a letter to Jane. (의문문으로)
   → _____

8. It was cold in Paris. (의문문으로)
   → _____

Exercise 1 | 다음 명사의 복수형을 쓰시오.

1. house → _____
2. city → _____
3. tomato → _____
4. knife → _____
5. bench → _____
6. leaf → _____
7. toy → _____
8. foot → _____
9. piano → _____
10. candy → _____
11. deer → _____
12. ball → _____
13. baby → _____
14. fox → _____
15. robot → _____
16. wolf → _____
17. woman → _____
18. dress → _____

Exercise 2 | 다음 주어진 명사의 복수형을 넣어 문장을 완성하시오.

1. He likes _____. (potato)

2. They have many _____. (friend)

3. There are four _____ in the field. (sheep)

4. The _____ sleep on the grass. (ox)

5. All the _____ are blue in this town. (roof)

6. _____ have big mouths. (hippo)

7. _____ are skating on the ice. (child)

8. There are some dirty _____. (glove)

9. She buys many _____. (fish)

10. Five _____ are on the hill. (man)

다음 괄호 안에서 알맞은 것을 고르시오.

1. (a / an) actress
2. (a / an) backpack
3. (a / an) lion
4. (a / an) orange
5. (a / an) scientist
6. (a / an) university
7. (a / an) rose
8. (a / an) octopus
9. (a / an) police officer
10. (a / an) egg
11. (a / an) hour
12. (a / an) umbrella
13. (a / an) onion
14. (a / an) chair
15. (a / an) European
16. (a / an) MP3 player
17. (a / an) old ball
18. (a / an) honest girl

다음 문장의 빈칸에 the를 쓰고, 필요 없는 곳은 ×표 하시오.

1. He plays _____ guitar very well.

2. They meet my friend on _____ Friday.

3. I have _____ lunch at noon.

4. Let's go to _____ south.

5. He plays _____ baseball with his friends.

6. I go to _____ bed at ten o'clock.

7. Julie plays _____ cello every day.

8. The earth goes around _____ sun.

9. She goes to the station by _____ bus.

10. There are _____ monkeys in the zoo.

Chapter 4. 동사의 시제

Exercise 1 다음 주어진 동사를 사용하여 현재진행형 문장을 완성하시오.

1. He _____ the violin. (play)

2. She and I _____ milk. (drink)

3. It _____ in New York. (rain)

4. I _____ a letter. (write)

5. Brian _____ his mom. (help)

6. She _____ a new jacket. (wear)

7. We _____ luggage. (carry)

8. Some children _____ soccer. (play)

9. The man _____ to the party. (come)

10. My mom _____ a song. (sing)

Exercise 2 다음 문장을 지시대로 바꿔 쓰시오.

1. The rabbit jumps high. (현재진행형 의문문으로)
   → _____

2. I listen to music. (현재진행형 부정문으로)
   → _____

3. He sleeps on the bed. (현재진행형 의문문으로)
   → _____

4. They look at the elephant. (현재진행형 의문문으로)
   → _____

5. She cooks in the kitchen. (현재진행형 부정문으로)
   → _____

6. It snows a lot in Seoul. (현재진행형 의문문으로)
   → _____

7. He swims in the pool. (현재진행형 의문문으로)
   → _____

8. She and he watch the movie. (현재진행형 부정문으로)
   → _____

Exercise 3 | 다음 주어진 말을 이용하여 미래형 문장으로 다시 쓰시오.

1. He brings you the book. (be going to)
   → _____

2. She waits for you at the playground. (will)
   → _____

3. Ann sends an e-mail to him. (be going to)
   → _____

4. My mother cleans my room. (will)
   → _____

5. The woman makes some cookies. (will)
   → _____

6. I keep a diary in my room. (be going to)
   → _____

7. Joseph plays computer games. (will)
   → _____

Exercise 4 | 다음 문장을 지시대로 바꿔 쓰시오.

1. He will fly a kite on the hill. (의문문으로)
   → _____

2. We are going to use paper cups. (부정문으로, 축약형)
   → _____

3. You are going to visit your parents. (의문문으로)
   → _____

4. He will be a famous musician. (의문문으로)
   → _____

5. She will go to the concert next month. (부정문으로, 축약형)
   → _____

6. This movie is going to end in five minutes. (부정문으로, 축약형)
   → _____

7. They are going to arrive here tomorrow. (의문문으로)
   → _____

Exercise 1 다음 주어진 단어들을 배열하여 문장을 완성하시오.

1. does / what / your father / do / ?
   → _____

2. you / at the station / do / who / meet / ?
   → _____

3. does / he / come / why / late / ?
   → _____

4. Emily / does / what / bring / ?
   → _____

5. does / where / live / Tom / ?
   → _____

6. do / when / read / you / books / ?
   → _____

Exercise 2 다음 질문에 대한 알맞은 대답을 고르시오.

1. Where is my backpack?
   ① It is under the table.   ② It's mine.

2. How is she today?
   ① She is in the room.   ② She is fine.

3. Why does he get up late?
   ① He gets up at six.   ② Because he is tired.

4. Where do the boys go?
   ① They go to the museum.   ② Because it rains.

5. How does she go to the library?
   ① She goes there on foot.   ② She goes there at ten.

6. Where do camels live?
   ① They live in the desert.   ② They are very good.

7. When does the show start?
   ① Because it starts.   ② It starts at seven.

8. How does she go to Busan?
   ① She goes there by train.   ② She works there.

9. Why does the girl cry?
   ① She waits for my father.   ② Because the movie is sad.

Exercise 3 | 다음 질문에 대한 알맞은 대답을 주어+동사가 있는 완전한 문장으로 쓰시오.

1. Where do you go after school? (to the theater)
   → _____

2. Why are you laughing? (this book is funny)
   → _____

3. When does she leave for London? (tomorrow)
   → _____

4. Who is Jenny looking at? (Tom)
   → _____

5. What is Peter making now? (a model car)
   → _____

6. How do you go to the zoo? (by subway)
   → _____

7. What does she have in her hands? (some coins)
   → _____

Exercise 4 | 다음 대답을 참고하여 괄호 안에서 알맞은 것을 고르시오.

1. How (old, often) is your sister?
   - She is nine years old.

2. How (tall, far) is Seoul from here?
   - It's 40 kilometers.

3. How (much, many) meals do you eat a day?
   - I have three meals a day.

4. How (often, far) do you go to the gym?
   - I go to the gym twice a week.

5. How (old, tall) is the tree?
   - It's 15 meters tall.

6. How (many, long) is the ruler?
   - It's 30 centimeters long.

7. How (far, long) do you play tennis?
   - I play tennis for one hour.

8. How (tall, often) is your little brother?
   - He is 130 centimeters tall.

Exercise 1 다음 주어진 조동사를 넣어 문장을 다시 쓰시오.

1. The girl plays the piano. (can)
   → _____

2. Mike is in his room. (may)
   → _____

3. She goes to see a doctor. (have to)
   → _____

4. The man swims in the sea. (be able to)
   → _____

5. They are in the classroom. (must)
   → _____

6. My brother and I leave this town. (will)
   → _____

7. They meet their mom. (be going to)
   → _____

Exercise 2 다음 문장을 부정문으로 바꿔 쓰시오.

1. My sister can ride a bike.
   → _____

2. You must write a letter to her. (금지)
   → _____

3. Lisa is able to drive a car.
   → _____

4. He can cook the Italian food.
   → _____

5. Mr. Brown may be late again.
   → _____

6. Ann is going to wait for him.
   → _____

7. We have to meet her in the library. (불필요)
   → _____

8. We will buy a present for him.
   → _____

다음 주어진 조동사를 사용하여 의문문으로 바꿔 쓰시오.

1. She uses a computer well. (can)
   → _____

2. Her brother plays basketball. (be able to)
   → _____

3. I take a picture in the museum. (may)
   → _____

4. You clean your room this evening. (be going to)
   → _____

5. I use your dictionary. (can)
   → _____

6. Your father plays badminton well. (be able to)
   → _____

7. You come to my birthday party. (will)
   → _____

다음 문장에서 틀린 부분을 바르게 고쳐 다시 쓰시오.

1. Tony can uses chopsticks.
   → _____

2. It mays rains next Monday.
   → _____

3. Are you able to helping the poor boy?
   → _____

4. She must are very angry.
   → _____

5. You doesn't have to wear a big hat.
   → _____

6. The child have to brush the teeth.
   → _____

7. He must gets up early tomorrow.
   → _____

8. Mina's brother cans fix the bench.
   → _____

Exercise 1   다음 문장에서 형용사를 찾아 동그라미 하시오.

1. The teacher is very kind.

2. I am tired and thirsty.

3. He is a famous painter.

4. This is his new white car.

5. I eat some cakes at the restaurant.

6. Her teddy bears are so pretty.

7. It is very sweet chocolate.

8. They are his young daughters.

9. The house is big and beautiful.

10. The handsome men are her brothers.

Exercise 2   다음 문장의 괄호 안에서 알맞은 것을 고르시오.

1. She reads the book (slow, slowly).

2. I ate food (full, fully) last night.

3. The movie is (pretty, prettily) scared.

4. My mom and dad smile (happy, happily).

5. My grandma speaks (loud, loudly).

6. I arrived at the station (late, lately).

7. The birds fly (high, highly) in the sky.

8. Listen to your teacher (careful, carefully).

9. Every student solves the problem (easy, easily).

10. He plays computer games (good, well).

다음 주어진 빈도부사를 넣어 문장을 다시 쓰시오.

1. John doesn't eat onions. (often)
   → _____

2. The bus isn't late. (usually)
   → _____

3. She is in the library. (sometimes)
   → _____

4. Do you walk to school? (always)
   → _____

5. Jenny goes to the concert. (often)
   → _____

6. She can remember his name. (never)
   → _____

7. This bookstore closes at ten. (usually)
   → _____

8. They are very busy. (always)
   → _____

다음 우리말과 같도록 빈칸에 알맞은 말을 쓰시오.

1. Jane is _____ Amy. (tall)
   Jane은 Amy보다 더 키가 크다.

2. Kate is _____ an actress. (popular)
   Kate는 배우만큼 인기가 많다.

3. She is _____ her sister. (beautiful)
   그녀는 그녀의 여동생보다 더 아름답다.

4. Grandmother is _____ in my family. (old)
   할머니는 우리 가족 중에서 가장 나이가 많으시다.

5. Tom is _____ Judy. (smart)
   Tom은 Judy만큼 영리하다.

6. This building is _____ in the city. (big)
   이 건물이 그 도시에서 가장 크다.

7. That apple is _____ this orange. (sweet)
   저 사과는 이 오렌지만큼 달지 않다.

Exercise 1 다음 문장을 지시대로 바꿔 쓰시오.

1. You are kind to everyone. (명령문으로)
   → _____

2. We go camping this Sunday. (제안문으로)
   → _____

3. You run in the classroom. (부정명령문으로)
   → _____

4. You open the window. (부정명령문으로)
   → _____

5. You brush your teeth. (명령문으로)
   → _____

6. We go to Jane's birthday party. (제안문으로)
   → _____

7. We pick the flowers. (부정제안문으로)
   → _____

8. You have a nice day. (명령문으로)
   → _____

Exercise 2 다음 문장의 괄호 안에서 알맞은 것을 고르시오.

1. (What, How) a pretty woman she is!

2. (What, How) greedy they are!

3. (What, How) poor the cat is!

4. (What, How) a rich man he is!

5. (What, How) cute the baby is!

6. (What, How) a fine day!

7. (What, How) easy books they are!

8. (What, How) smart he is!

9. (What, How) strong the man is!

10. (What, How) hot coffee this is!

Exercise 3 | 다음 문장을 감탄문으로 바꿔 쓰시오.

1. This book is very difficult. (how)
   → _____

2. His hands are very dirty. (how)
   → _____

3. This is a very wonderful house. (what)
   → _____

4. They are very hungry. (how)
   → _____

5. She is a very great actress. (what)
   → _____

6. They are very nice dresses. (what)
   → _____

7. The woman is very famous. (how)
   → _____

8. These are very big cakes. (what)
   → _____

Exercise 4 | 다음 문장의 괄호 안에서 알맞은 것을 고르시오.

1. Your house is very big, (is, isn't) it?

2. Tom and Dan don't like pizza, (does, do) they?

3. Sally found her wallet, (did, didn't) she?

4. They won't go hiking, (will, won't) they?

5. Richard doesn't drink coffee, (do, does) he?

6. Jason caught the thief, (doesn't, didn't) he?

7. Her brother broke the mirror, didn't (he, she)?

8. Joe was late for the meeting, (was, wasn't) he?

9. They were your friends, (aren't, weren't) they?

10. He can count the number of lambs, (can, can't) he?

Exercise 1 다음 주어진 동사를 to부정사로 바꿔 쓰시오.

1. She was pleased _____ her mother. (see)

2. _____ novels is interesting. (read)

3. It is very boring _____ history. (study)

4. I want _____ a painter. (am)

5. The boy went there _____ a toy. (buy)

6. My dream is _____ a teacher. (is)

7. I am so happy _____ you. (meet)

8. It is very important _____ to school. (go)

9. We decided _____ a taxi. (take)

10. He was sorry _____ the news. (hear)

Exercise 2 다음 우리말과 같도록 빈칸에 알맞은 말을 쓰시오.

1. 나는 너에게 줄 것이 아무것도 없다. (give)
   I have nothing _____ _____ you.

2. 그 소녀들은 집으로 돌아가기를 원했다. (go)
   The girls wanted _____ _____ back home.

3. 사람들이 그의 그림을 좋아하기 시작했다. (like)
   People started _____ _____ his paintings.

4. 그녀는 그녀의 일을 끝마쳐서 기뻤다. (finish)
   She was pleased _____ _____ her work.

5. 많은 아이들이 콜라 마시는 것을 좋아한다. (drink)
   Many kids like _____ _____ Coke.

6. 모든 식물들은 살기 위해서 물이 필요하다. (live)
   All the plants need water _____ _____.

7. 나는 피아노 수업을 듣고 싶다. (take)
   I'd like _____ _____ piano lessons.

8. 당신은 떠날 계획이 있나요? (leave)
   Do you have any plans _____ _____?

다음 문장의 괄호 안에서 알맞은 것을 고르시오.

1. Her hobby is (surf, surfing) the Internet.

2. Thank you for (to come, coming).

3. Jim gave up (to take, taking) the math test.

4. My job is (sell, selling) cars in this city.

5. (Keep, Keeping) a diary is not easy.

6. We always enjoy (to listen, listening) to music.

7. He continued (lose, to lose) the game.

8. How about (to jog, jogging) in the morning?

9. The students wanted (to see, seeing) the people.

10. Many people enjoy (to ski, skiing) in winter.

다음 주어진 동사를 활용해서 빈칸에 알맞은 형태로 쓰시오.

1. He never gives up _____ a job. (get)

2. We kept _____ the fence. (paint)

3. She wants _____ the new shoes. (buy)

4. He avoids _____ a big dog. (meet)

5. Jack decided _____ the building. (buy)

6. Did he finish _____ the newspaper? (read)

7. They didn't plan _____ the window. (break)

8. Nancy can't stop _____ him. (love)

9. He needs _____ a letter to her. (write)

10. I hope _____ around the world. (travel)

Exercise 1 | 다음 문장의 괄호 안에서 알맞은 것을 고르시오.

1. There (is, are) an eraser in the pencil case.

2. There (is, are) four clerks in the store.

3. There (is, are) a dog on the sofa.

4. There (is, are) some flour in the bowl.

5. There (is, are) many mountains in Korea.

6. There (is, are) a printer between the computers.

7. There (is, are) an oven in the dining room.

8. There (is, are) three pillows on the bed.

9. There (is, are) a lot of food in the refrigerator.

10. There (is, are) a bicycle in the yard.

Exercise 2 | 다음 문장의 괄호 안에서 알맞은 것을 고르시오.

1. The room smelled very (terrible, terribly).

2. The oranges taste (sour, sourly).

3. The flowers look (beautiful, beautifully).

4. The cloth feels (smooth, smoothly).

5. This bell sounds (sweet, sweetly).

6. Mr. Brown teaches (us math, math us).

7. Sue made sandwiches (for, of) the kids.

8. She lends a ball (to, for) him.

9. She asked their names (to, of) the students.

10. Please pass the sugar (to, of) me.

다음 문장을 3형식 문장으로 바꿔 쓰시오.

1. He always asks us difficult questions.
   → _____

2. We made Lisa a big chocolate cake.
   → _____

3. Daniel bought his mom a yellow scarf.
   → _____

4. My sister showed them her pictures.
   → _____

5. Peter buys his cousin an interesting book.
   → _____

6. Mr. Johnson taught them history.
   → _____

7. My aunt cooked her daughter spaghetti.
   → _____

8. Tony wrote his friend an e-mail.
   → _____

다음 문장의 빈칸에 주어진 말을 알맞은 형태로 바꿔 쓰시오.

1. She asked me _____ a doctor. (see)

2. These candies tastes _____. (delicious)

3. I wanted you _____ home early. (come)

4. This water feels very _____. (cold)

5. They told the girl _____ up. (cheer)

6. Dan asked a lot of questions _____. (her)

7. His voice sounds _____. (strange)

8. My uncle made a big kite _____. (me)

9. They allow him _____ to the party. (go)

10. Your hamsters look _____. (cute)

Exercise 1

다음 빈칸에 알맞은 전치사를 쓰시오.

1. ~ 쪽으로	_____	2. ~을 위해	_____
3. ~을 가지고	_____	4. ~의	_____
5. (일요일)에	_____	6. (5월)에	_____
7. (방학) 동안	_____	8. ~ 위로	_____
9. (2시간) 동안	_____	10. ~로부터	_____
11. ~ 안에	_____	12. ~ 위에	_____
13. ~ 옆에	_____	14. ~ 뒤에	_____
15. ~ 아래에	_____	16. (오후)에	_____
17. (4시)에	_____	18. (가을)에	_____
19. (밤)에	_____	20. (서울)에	_____

Exercise 2

다음 문장의 괄호 안에서 알맞은 것을 고르시오.

1. The cat is (in, under) the chair.

2. The refrigerator is (to, next to) the table.

3. The clock is (at, on) the wall.

4. The shop closes (at, in) ten o'clock.

5. We have many holidays (in, on) May.

6. I work (on, from) Monday to Friday.

7. This cap is (to, for) my son.

8. He was born (at, in) 2007.

9. (On, In) the afternoon, I play soccer.

10. My birthday is (at, on) October 31st.

다음 문장의 괄호 안에서 알맞은 것을 고르시오.

1. Peter is (about, in) his office.

2. A sofa is (through, in front of) the table.

3. A big garden is (across from, during) the house.

4. It is (along, between) the bank and the bakery.

5. A squirrel is running (up, about) the tree.

6. A mouse comes (out of, of) the closet.

7. He and she walk (before, around) the street.

8. They often eat ice cream (on, in) summer.

9. My brother goes to school (by, with) bus.

10. Lucy has lunch (with, about) her mother.

다음 우리말과 같도록 빈칸에 알맞은 말을 쓰시오.

1. There is a deer _____ the big tree.
   그 큰 나무 옆에 사슴 한 마리가 있다.

2. His father makes a model car _____ his son.
   그의 아버지는 그의 아들을 위해 모형 차를 만든다.

3. They lived _____ the beach.
   그들은 해변 근처에 살았다.

4. The school begins _____ March.
   그 학교는 3월에 시작한다.

5. I play soccer _____ friends _____ Saturdays.
   나는 토요일마다 친구들과 함께 축구를 한다.

6. My parents take a walk _____ the evening.
   나의 부모님은 저녁에 산책을 하신다.

7. We run _____ here _____ the park.
   우리는 여기서 그 공원까지 달려간다.

8. Jennifer leaves _____ New York.
   Jennifer는 뉴욕을 향해 떠난다.

Exercise 1 다음 문장의 괄호 안에서 알맞은 것을 고르시오.

1. I wash my hands first (but, before) I eat food.

2. (After, So) you do your homework, watch TV.

3. Do you want juice (but, or) milk?

4. My mother is sick, (but, so) she is in the hospital.

5. I like apples, (and, when) my sister likes oranges.

6. He was surprised (or, when) he met the actor.

7. I have a cold, (but, or) my brother doesn't.

8. I have no money, (but, so) I can't buy the car.

9. She was young, (and, but) she was very brave.

10. I lived in the country (what, when) I was young.

Exercise 2 다음 〈보기〉에서 알맞은 것을 골라 문장의 빈칸에 쓰시오.

〈보기〉 and   but   or   so   because

1. She is very tall, _____ her sister is short.

2. We like Alice _____ she is kind.

3. This doll is pretty _____ expensive.

4. His brother broke his robot, _____ he is angry.

5. You can answer yes, _____ no.

6. We had to study, _____ we went to the library.

7. Cathy has two dogs _____ four hamsters.

8. Jill is beautiful, smart, _____ diligent.

9. Do you want iced coffee, _____ hot coffee?

10. I went to the dentist _____ I had a toothache.

Exercise 3 | 다음 〈보기〉에서 알맞은 것을 골라 문장의 빈칸에 쓰시오.

| 〈보기〉 | before | after | when | that | if | because |

1. My hair was curly _____ I was young.
   ~ 할 때

2. I don't know _____ Daniel left New York.
   ~하는 것

3. He made a wish _____ he blew out the candle.
   ~하기 전에

4. I bought sneakers _____ I saved some money.
   ~한 후에

5. He can eat cookies _____ he wants to eat them.
   ~한다면

6. We closed the window _____ it was cold.
   ~ 때문에

Exercise 4 | 다음 주어진 단어를 이용하여 한 문장으로 쓰시오.

1. Sally is tired. She is sick. (and)
   → _____

2. Mom bought a magazine. She didn't read it. (but)
   → _____

3. We can tell the truth. We can tell a lie. (or)
   → _____

4. We have lunch. We are still hungry. (but)
   → _____

5. I went to the window. I looked out. (and)
   → _____

6. My father has five dogs. He has ten pigs. (and)
   → _____

7. Are those rabbits yours? Are those rabbits hers? (or)
   → _____

8. He knows the answer. He didn't tell her. (but)
   → _____

Chapter 1. be동사와 대명사

Exercise 1>

1. He isn't an artist.
2. They aren't farmers.
3. It isn't our house.
4. She isn't his sister.
5. Her daughter isn't very tall.
6. My father isn't in the hospital.
7. We aren't twelve years old.
8. He isn't tired and sleepy.

Exercise 2>

1. Are you busy?
2. Is she from Canada?
3. Are the children in the park?
4. Are you a good singer?
5. Are they interesting?
6. Are the stores open today?
7. Are John and Ann cooks?

Exercise 3>

1. your 2. They 3. My 4. it 5. We 6. her 7. him
8. them 9. They 10. me

Exercise 4>

1. This 2. these 3. Those are 4. Those watches
5. This is 6. Those books 7. This ring
8. These rooms 9. It is 10. These flowers

Chapter 2. 일반동사

Exercise 1>

1. cries 2. play 3. washes 4. has 5. rains 6. wants
7. come 8. walk 9. fall 10. does

Exercise 2>

1. saw 2. ate 3. had 4. were 5. met 6. bought
7. built 8. went 9. was 10. made

Exercise 3>

1. don't like 2. doesn't drink 3. don't want
4. doesn't have 5. doesn't teach 6. Do you speak
7. Does Amy study 8. Do you choose
9. Do they carry 10. Do Jim and you leave

Exercise 4>

1. He didn't read a newspaper yesterday.
2. My father wasn't a firefighter.
3. We didn't go to the market.
4. Brian didn't do his homework.
5. Were you late for school then?
6. Did Ann visit her uncle?
7. Did he send a letter to Jane?
8. Was it cold in Paris?

Chapter 3. 명사와 관사

Exercise 1>

1. houses 2. cities 3. tomatoes 4. knives 5. benches
6. leaves 7. toys 8. feet 9. pianos 10. candies
11. deer 12. balls 13. babies 14. foxes 15. robots
16. wolves 17. women 18. dresses

Exercise 2>

1. potatoes 2. friends 3. sheep 4. oxen 5. roofs
6. Hippos 7. Children 8. gloves 9. fish 10. men

Exercise 3>

1. an 2. a 3. a 4. an 5. a 6. a 7. a 8. an 9. a
10. an 11. an 12. an 13. an 14. a 15. a 16. an
17. an 18. an

Exercise 4>

1. the 2. × 3. × 4. the 5. × 6. × 7. the 8. the
9. × 10. ×

Chapter 4. 동사의 시제

Exercise 1>

1. is playing 2. are drinking 3. is raining
4. am writing 5. is helping 6. is wearing
7. are carrying 8. are playing 9. is coming
10. is singing

Exercise 2>

1. Is the rabbit jumping high?
2. I'm[I am] not listening to music.
3. Is he sleeping on the bed?
4. Are they looking at the elephant?

5. She isn't[is not] cooking in the kitchen.

6. Is it snowing a lot in Seoul?

7. Is he swimming in the pool?

8. She and he aren't[are not] watching the movie.

Exercise 3>

1. He is going to bring you the book.

2. She will wait for you at the playground.

3. Ann is going to send an e-mail to him.

4. My mother will clean my room.

5. The woman will make some cookies.

6. I am going to keep a diary in my room.

7. Joseph will play computer games.

Exercise 4>

1. Will he fly a kite on the hill?

2. We aren't going to use paper cups.

3. Are you going to visit your parents?

4. Will he be a famous musician?

5. She won't go to the concert next month.

6. This movie isn't going to end in five minutes.

7. Are they going to arrive here tomorrow?

Chapter 5. 의문사

Exercise 1>

1. What does your father do?

2. Who do you meet at the station?

3. Why does he come late?

4. What does Emily bring?

5. Where does Tom live?

6. When do you read books?

Exercise 2>

1. ① 2. ② 3. ② 4. ① 5. ① 6. ① 7. ② 8. ①

9. ②

Exercise 3>

1. I go to the theater after school.

2. I'm laughing because this book is funny.

3. She will leave for London tomorrow.

4. She is looking at Tom.

5. He is making a model car now.

6. I go to the zoo by subway.

7. She has some coins in her hands.

Exercise 4>

1. old 2. far 3. many 4. often 5. tall 6. long

7. long 8. tall

Chapter 6. 조동사

Exercise 1>

1. The girl can play the piano.

2. Mike may be in his room.

3. She has to go to see a doctor.

4. The man is able to swim in the sea.

5. They must be in the classroom.

6. My brother and I will leave this town.

7. They are going to meet their mom.

Exercise 2>

1. My sister can't ride a bike.

2. You must not write a letter to her.

3. Lisa isn't able to drive a car.

4. He can't cook the Italian food.

5. Mr. Brown may not be late again.

6. Ann isn't going to wait for him.

7. We don't have to meet her in the library.

8. We won't buy a present for him.

Exercise 3>

1. Can she use a computer well?

2. Is her brother able to play basketball?

3. May I take a picture in the museum?

4. Are you going to clean your room this evening?

5. Can I use your dictionary?

6. Is your father able to play badminton well?

7. Will you come to my birthday party?

Exercise 4>

1. Tony can use chopsticks.

2. It may rain next Monday.

3. Are you able to help the poor boy?

4. She must be very angry.

5. You don't have to wear a big hat.

6. The child has to brush the teeth.

7. He must get up early tomorrow.

8. Mina's brother can fix the bench.

Chapter 7. 형용사와 부사

Exercise 1>

1. kind 2. tired, thirsty 3. famous 4. new, white
5. some 6. pretty 7. sweet 8. young 9. big, beautiful
10. handsome

Exercise 2>

1. slowly 2. fully 3. pretty 4. happily 5. loudly
6. late 7. high 8. carefully 9. easily 10. well

Exercise 3>

1. John doesn't often eat onions.
2. The bus isn't usually late.
3. She is sometimes in the library.
4. Do you always walk to school?
5. Jenny often goes to the concert.
6. She can never remember his name.
7. This bookstore usually closes at ten.
8. They are always very busy.

Exercise 4>

1. taller than 2. as popular as 3. more beautiful than
4. the oldest 5. as smart as 6. the biggest
7. not as[so] sweet as

Chapter 8. 문장의 종류

Exercise 1>

1. Be kind to everyone.
2. Let's go camping this Sunday.
3. Don't run in the classroom.
4. Don't open the window.
5. Brush your teeth.
6. Let's go to Jane's birthday party.
7. Let's not pick the flowers.
8. Have a nice day.

Exercise 2>

1. What 2. How 3. How 4. What 5. How 6. What
7. What 8. How 9. How 10. What

Exercise 3>

1. How difficult this book is!
2. How dirty his hands are!
3. What a wonderful house this is!
4. How hungry they are!
5. What a great actress she is!
6. What nice dresses they are!
7. How famous the woman is!
8. What big cakes these are!

Exercise 4>

1. isn't 2. do 3. didn't 4. will 5. does 6. didn't
7. he 8. wasn't 9. weren't 10. can't

Chapter 9. to부정사와 동명사

Exercise 1>

1. to see 2. To read 3. to study 4. to be 5. to buy
6. to be 7. to meet 8. to go 9. to take 10. to hear

Exercise 2>

1. to, give 2. to, go 3. to, like 4. to, finish
5. to, drink 6. to, live 7. to, take 8. to, leave

Exercise 3>

1. surfing 2. coming 3. taking 4. selling 5. Keeping
6. listening 7. to lose 8. jogging 9. to see
10. skiing

Exercise 4>

1. getting 2. painting 3. to buy 4. meeting 5. to buy
6. reading 7. to break 8. loving 9. to write
10. to travel

Chapter 10. 문장의 형태

Exercise 1>

1. is 2. are 3. is 4. is 5. are 6. is 7. is 8. are
9. is 10. is

Exercise 2>

1. terrible 2. sour 3. beautiful 4. smooth 5. sweet
6. us math 7. for 8. to 9. of 10. to

Exercise 3>

1. He always asks difficult questions of us.
2. We made a big chocolate cake for Lisa.
3. Daniel bought a yellow scarf for his mom.
4. My sister showed her pictures to them.
5. Peter buys an interesting book for his cousin.
6. Mr. Johnson taught history to them.
7. My aunt cooked spaghetti for her daughter.
8. Tony wrote an e-mail to his friend.

Exercise 4>

1. to see 2. delicious 3. to come 4. cold
5. to cheer 6. of her 7. strange 8. for me
9. to go 10. cute

Chapter 11. 전치사

Exercise 1>

1. to 2. for 3. with 4. of 5. on 6. in 7. during
8. up 9. for 10. from 11. in 12. on 13. next to/by
14. behind 15. under 16. in 17. at 18. in 19. at
20. in

Exercise 2>

1. under 2. next to 3. on 4. at 5. in 6. from 7. for
8. in 9. In 10. on

Exercise 3>

1. in 2. in front of 3. across from 4. between 5. up
6. out of 7. around 8. in 9. by 10. with

Exercise 4>

1. next to/by 2. for 3. near 4. in 5. with, on 6. in
7. from, to 8. for

Chapter 12. 접속사

Exercise 1>

1. before 2. After 3. or 4. so 5. and 6. when
7. but 8. so 9. but 10. when

Exercise 2>

1. but 2. because 3. but 4. so 5. or 6. so 7. and
8. and 9. or 10. because

Exercise 3>

1. when 2. that 3. before 4. after 5. if 6. because

Exercise 4>

1. Sally is tired and (she is) sick.
2. Mom bought a magazine, but she didn't read it.
3. We can tell the truth or (tell) a lie.
4. We have lunch, but we are still hungry.
5. I went to the window and looked out.
6. My father has five dogs and ten pigs.
7. Are those rabbits yours or hers?
8. He knows the answer, but he didn't tell her.

Let's Study!
The **Grammar School** 예비중학

새로운 중학교 교과 과정 반영
자기주도 학습을 통한 내신 완벽 대비
내신 기출 문제 분석, 명확한 핵심 문법 해설
Workbook – 다양하고 풍부한 문법문제 수록

The **Grammar School** 예비중학
The **Grammar School** 1 중학
The **Grammar School** 2 중학
The **Grammar School** 3 중학

Iam books
문의전화 02-6343-0999